MW01295053

I PROBABLY SCREWED YOU TOO!
The Mostly True Story of Kenny Bolin

By Kenny Bolin
With John Cosper

Copyright 2015 by Bolin Services

Cover designed by Christopher J. Longenecker

Art work on the white cover by Travis Heckel

This book is dedicated to my other son, Rico Costantino, whom I apparently had when I was just a year old.

"Dammit, Kenny, I've heard this story before!"
Jim Cornette

"Now hold on, hear me out, the ending may have changed."
Kenny Bolin

AN OPEN LETTER TO MR. BOLIN

You and Cornette were funny. I was listening to it and trying to figure out how I would hang in that improv. You guys are, I assume, Jerry Lawler students, which is to say like wrestling Henny Youngman. You have an encyclopedic vault of the vaudevillian-like one liners, insults, and toss them back and forth with ease in addition to your own spin.

I remember telling you years ago that you guys did that shit so well, like Abbot and Costello "Who's on first?" that you worked me. Of course, now older, more washed up, and wiser. I just marvel at the chemistry. Shit, Kenny, with Cornette, [Paul] Heyman, and Bobby [Heenan] off the national radar for several years there, I thought of myself as the big fish in the small pond of managers until I heard you. With all due respect, I'm glad the great unwashed masses didn't get to directly compare you to me.

Although I had more of a national presence, you got to work consistently more than I ever did, managed far better talent than I ever did, and were allowed to be the lovable con artist you are without any obvious outside "producing" and "writing" to spoil your unique personality.

To steal a phrase from Hunter S. Thompson, you are "one of God's own prototypes." I really am astounded you didn't get picked up. I would have loved to hear you do color over the goofy bullshit I did through the years. I am envious of your career.

That salad tossing is on the house, my friend. Now go swindle somebody.

James Mitchell
aka, "Sinister Minister"
February 15, 2015

A MESSAGE FROM DIRTY DUTCH MANTELL

The name of the book... **I PROBABLY SCREWED YOU TOO** is an understatement for this rag of a manuscript. The term SCREW doesn't come close to what damage Bolin has done not only to me and countless others but to the wrestling profession as a whole. Kenny Bolin... **if that is his real name**...is to the wrestling business what the bubonic plague was to Europe in the 14th century that killed an estimated 25 million people. Of course, Bolin could kill that many with one interview. I never found out how Bolin actually conned his way into the wrestling profession but due to my watching hundreds of detective shows, I've deduced that somehow Jimmy Cornette is involved in this travesty in some form. Bolin has been known to kill complete wrestling shows just by being advertised on the card.

Usually, to get into this business, it requires somewhat of a monetary investment but seeing as how Bolin is tighter than the rope that hung Saddam Hussein, that theory is cast in doubt. But Cornette or whoever allowed Kenny Bolin to enter a wrestling show without buying a ticket should have gotten something. I suggest somewhere in the range of 3 to 5 grand...oh I'm sorry...I meant to say 3 to 5. YEARS!!! IN PRISON!!! Maximum security too such as GITMO.

I was contacted to give my true feelings on Kenny Bolin for this book...because there needs to be, at least, some truth in this crappy book because everybody knows that Bolin has never spoke a true statement in his life. Bolin has told more lies than Bill Clinton told Hillary about Monica Lewinsky. You know how to tell Kenny Bolin is lying? If his mouth is open, he's lying. I once heard an overweight middle aged woman say that she would like to throw her arms around Bolin and hug him but she didn't have arms like an orangutan so that would be impossible. Seriously, Bolin has had a tough life stemming from his childhood days. Not a lot of people know this but Bolin was an unwanted child. So unwanted in fact that his mother left young Kenny the day **BEFORE** he was born. The only difference between a wet dog and Kenny Bolin… is… WATER.

OK so the pleasantries are over.Seriously speaking, I've known Kenny for a long time. I first met Kenny when the DEAD SEA was just sick. He's a good guy. That is if you don't mind knowing a psychopathic, lying, cheating, narcissistic, conniving backstabbing bastage. Other than those minor personality traits, he's great. Just watch your wallet.

Dirty Dutch
May 29, 2015

AND FINALLY, A WORD FROM JIM CORNETTE

Jim Cornette

Wrestling fans, I cannot tell you what an honor and privilege it is to write the introduction for Kenny Starmaker Bolin's long awaited autobiography. Normally, when folks ask me to write such things, I charge a king's ransom for my services, but for Kenny, I had to do it for free. Why? No, it's not because the Starmaker offered me a free pair of his high quality Beets by Bolin headphones with the optional microphone cable and my beloved Louisville Cardinals logo on the side. It's because I wouldn't be where I am today, charging a king's ransom for my endorsements, if it were not for Kenny Bolin.

Kenny Bolin is the man who taught me everything I know about the business of wrestling. Everything from my brightly colored suits to my loaded tennis racket was copied off Bolin. Even the fiery way in which I cut my promos is but a pale copy - dare I say, a shadow - of my oldest and dearest friend Kenny.

But Kenny is more than just my idol, my hero, and my inspiration in the ring. Kenny Bolin was the best man at all of my weddings. He's the man responsible for teaching me how to be a great booker. He taught me everything I know about calling matches for television. He taught me how to mold the minds of young men and women into great wrestlers. He taught me how to shop for everything from stereo equipment to the perfect cut of meat. He introduced me to my long lost son, Little Jimmy LeBeau. And yes, ladies and gentlemen, Kenny Bolin taught me what a screw job is.

My only regret in this life is that, as a Cornette male, I will die young while my dear friend Kenny, based in his family history, will live well past 100. How I wish I could be there at the end, to stand in front of the mourning, weeping thousands, and sing to the world that Kenny Bolin was, is, and forever will be the Wing Beneath My Wings.

Signed,

James E. Cornette

June 1, 2015

A legal disclaimer from attorney Tim Denison

The authenticity of this introduction has been brought into question by Jim Cornette. Per an investigation by my office, this introduction was sent to co-author John Cosper via email by Mr. Bolin on June 1, 2015. My client, Mr. Bolin claims it was emailed to him by my other client, Mr. Cornette and then forwarded on to Mr. Cosper. Given that Mr. Cornette and Mr. Cosper are both friends outside of their connection to Mr. Bolin, it is suspicious that Mr. Cornette would send this material to Mr. Cosper by way of Mr. Bolin. However, after obtaining a writing sample from Mr. Bolin, my office concluded with absolute certainty that it was not written by Mr. Bolin, whose writing sample was so rife with errors in grammar, punctuation, spelling, and capitalization, an expert in the field of linguistics deemed it not only to be below second grade proficiency but, and I quote, "a crime against the English language."

My best legal advice to you, the reader, is to have fun with it and not take anything you are about to read too seriously. This is after all the MOSTLY true stories of Kenny Bolin, so those of you who are interested in truth would be wise to put this book down and go read some Plato. You might find truth, but you won't be near as entertained.

This page left intentionally blank...

So it will seem like the book is longer than it actually is.

If you think that's a bit dishonest, I refer you to the title on the cover of this book.

THE BOLIN FAMILY, OR THE PEOPLE RESPONSIBLE FOR WHO I BECAME

I was born on March 16, 1960 in Lexington, Kentucky. Contrary to popular legend, Ma Bolin was not visited by three wise men from the East on the day of my birth. In truth three men from Vince McMahon, Sr.'s WWWF did show up at the hospital that day bearing gifts, but they were sent to the wrong room. They had come to see Buddy Rogers, who was hospitalized in Lexington at the time with a mysterious ailment.

My family moved to LaGrange, Kentucky when I was two. My mother, Marie Bolin Rison, was married to Johnny Rison. You may not have heard the name, but Johnny Rison is a significant figure in my home state's history. He was the last man ever convicted of cattle rustling in Kentucky.

I remember being in the courtroom when Johnny Rison was convicted. We had to sit through another criminal case first. A man was accused of murdering his brother when he caught his brother in bed with the first man's wife. The man was convicted and sentenced to a mere eight months probation.

Upon hearing the verdict, I breathed a sigh of relief. Cattle rustling wasn't nearly as bad as murder, and there was only one cow. What's more, my step-dad wasn't even the real cattle rustler. He just happened to be with the guilty party when the cow was rustled.

Needless to say, we were all a little shocked when the judge sentenced Johnny Rison to eight *years.* Ma Bolin ran out of the courtroom crying. Luckily, Johnny only had to serve eight months before coming home to us.

Johnny was always on the move, and he moved our family to fourteen different homes in twelve years. I went to first grade at Crestwood Elementary, second grade at Ballardsville, third and fourth at LaGrange, fifth and sixth at Liberty, seventh & eighth at Oldham County Middle School, and four years of high school at Oldham County High School. I may not remember much of what I was taught, but hey, I was doing pretty well to remember where I was!

It was no small feat moving our family from point to point all those years because there were quite a few of us. I had three sisters, Deana, Janice, and June. I also had two step-sisters, Karen and Stacey. I also had one brother Timmy John, whom I didn't meet until later in life. Timmy John had a million nicknames, but only one good idea in his entire life. More on both of those facts later.

"Wait a minute, Mr. Bolin? Your last name is Rison? And you have step-sisters? Did I miss something?" Yes you did, and so did I! Until the age of 19, I believed Johnny Rison was my father and I was born in St. Petersburg, Florida. The truth is I was not Johnny Rison's son. My real father was Ray L. Stallings of Chesapeake, Virginia. Yes, long before I entered the business, my life had all the twists and turns of a Monday Night Raw episode, minus the mewling and screeching of Stephanie McMahon.

I only met Ray twice, once when I was nineteen and another time when my son, the Prince, was sixteen months old. I kept Johnny Rison's last name a while longer, but at age 26, I took back my birth name.

My first encounter with Ray proved to be a fortunate one. Ray knew I was a wrestling fan, and the night I arrived, he took me to the arena to see the man himself, Ric Flair. I had a scrapbook on my lap of photos taken by my dear "friend," Jim Cornette. An elderly man sitting next to me asked to look through it and began pointing out wrestlers whom he himself had faced.

That's when I realized who he was. "You're Lou Thesz!"

Lou was impressed with the photography work. I told Lou that the next time he was in Louisville, I would gladly hook him up with Cornette to do some photos. Just another favor I did for Jim Cornette that he would piss on later in life.

Jim Cornette

Kenny met Lou Thesz. That part is true. But the stuff about hooking me up to take Lou Thesz's picture never happened. Believe me I would remember!

Kenny

The one constant in my life growing up was my mother, dear old Ma Bolin. I'd love to tell you that Ma Bolin was the June Cleaver type, the perfect housewife who kept her house in order, saw the kids off to school, and waited dotingly for father to come home. She was not.

Ma was a fan of men in uniform. And men who drove trucks. And many other kinds of men. When we lived in Florida, Ma's dance card was full just about every night with the boys from the nearby naval base. Back in Kentucky, Ma got herself a CB radio and reached out to the truckers. I can't tell you the number of times I'd play back a tape of a wrestling show I'd recorded on my Betamax VCR only to hear "Kentucky Rose" reaching out to touch someone over the CB air waves.

Ma's extracurricular activities made for an interesting birthday for my sister Deena many years later. After asking Deena how old she was, she replied she was fifty-one.

"No," I said, "You are not."

Deena insisted she was fifty-one. I told her again she wasn't. She insisted her birthdate was March 17, 1959. I informed her she was born on March 17... 1957.

Deena was stunned. She had not only lost two years of her life she thought she had, she now had an even bigger question: who was her father? Deena called Ma Bolin and confronted her. Ma confirmed that yes, Deena was born in 1957 and not 1959, but as for the father question, well, that's another matter. Ma thought and thought. She went back in her mind to those Ozzie and Harriett days of the late 1950s. The best she could do was narrow it down to three possibilities, all from the naval base in Florida.

Christopher Bolin, aka The Prince

Ma Bolin liked them all, but she really loved the sea men.

Kenny

Some of the biggest fights I witnessed back then were not on television. One night Jim and I were getting ready to go to Showcase Cinemas when we heard Ma Bolin and Janice screaming at each other in the other room. The screaming turned to slapping and hitting, and when we couldn't stand it any longer, we walked out to the living room to survey the scene.

Janice had my mom by the hair and was wailing away on Ma. Ma, however, had the advantage. She had managed to get hold of an extension cord and was whipping my sister with the foreign object. Bravely, I dove into the fray. I pulled them apart and yanked the extension cord from Ma's hand.

I stepped out of the way and said, "Okay, wrestle!" They were right back at it, but they were fighting fair.

Jim Cornette

That apartment was a mess. It hadn't been renovated in at least fifty years. If you slapped the wall, dust would literally fly off the wall.

Kenny

Jim doesn't like messes. When he complained about the dust flying off the walls, I told him the solution was simple: don't hit the wall!

Jim Cornette

Kenny kept a padlock on his bedroom door to keep other people, in particular, his sister Janice's many, shady male friends, from touching his stuff. One hot summer he went and bought an air conditioner for his room, an air conditioner he did not share with his family.

One afternoon his mother and sister started pounding on the bedroom door, demanding that we let

17

them in. Kenny refused to open the door. Ma Bolin was furious, cussing and screaming at us. Kenny asked if she'd help pay the electricity bill for the air conditioner. She said no, so we didn't open the door.

Janice knocked next, begging us to let her and her one year old baby inside. We finally relented, but before we opened the door, we got into Kenny's closet and put on heavy coats and gloves. We opened the door, shivering and blowing on our hands to stay warm. Ma Bolin cussed us again as we grabbed the baby and shut the door.

We opened the door a second time a short while later. Ma Bolin hurled an RC bottle that just missed Kenny's head. Kenny smiled and said, "You missed!" just before he slammed it shut again.

Kenny

In all fairness I did offer Ma and Janice the opportunity to partake of my air conditioner when I got the unit. They declined to help pay the electric bill, so I never felt bad about keeping them out.

Janice and I got into a fight in that living room once. It ended when I shoved her face into the wall, knocking a face-shaped hole in the wall. We were terrified of what Ma Bolin would say. I got the bright idea to cover the spot with a picture frame. Was it cowardly? Yes. But Ma didn't discover the damage until years later - when she moved!

RUNNIN' WITH THE DEVIL, OR MY CHILDHOOD FRIEND JIM CORNETTE

Jim Cornette

I've told this story many times in personal appearances and on my podcast. Kenny and I met when we were teenagers at the Oldham County Fair. I was standing in line at the booth where you shoot the water in the clown's mouth. I reached in my back pocket to get my wallet to buy the tickets for the clown's mouth thing, and when I reached for my wallet in my pocket, I shook hands with Kenny Bolin.

Kenny and I hit it off right away. We always got together to watch wrestling, talk about wrestling, and read about wrestling. We'd take turns doing impressions of our favorites. Kenny did a great Lawler impression, and I could do a perfect Jimmy Valiant impression.

Kenny Bolin

Jimmy was a terrible Jimmy Valiant. He did a great Dusty Rhodes, and he could do a few others. But he was an awful Jimmy Valiant.

Cornette and I became the best of friends. We went to the weekly matches together, we watched wrestling on TV, and we spent all our free time talking wrestling. We were particularly fond of the wrestling publications back then, and Cornette would always go right to the wrestler rankings inside. He was a big Lawler fan, Cornette was, and he always wondered why Lawler could never reach that number one spot.

19

"They always put those east coast guys ahead of him!" Corny whined. "Did any of them see his match last week? Don't they know how good he is?"

"Jim," I said, "You know it's all fake, right?"

Jim's eyes bugged out from behind his specs so big, I thought they would crack the lenses. "What did you say?"

"Pro wrestling," I said. "It's all staged. It's pre-determined who will win and who will lose and how they will lose. It's nothing but a show."

"No," said Jim, tears welling up in his eyes. "Say it ain't so! Please, Kenny."
"Jim," I said. "You've been taking their photos for years. You mean you never knew it was fake?"

Jimmy said nothing. He sat their in stunned silence, his entire world possibly shattered.

John Cosper, wrestling historian

It should be noted here that the story just told was first told to me by Jim Cornette. It varies only slightly in that it was Kenny, not Jim, who was stunned to learn that professional wrestling was a work. Far be it from me to say who's story is phony, but it is a well known fact that Kenny was a huge Lawler fan growing up.

Kenny

Our home in LaGrange was a second story department over the LaGrange Fire Department. One day while I was at school, the fire department actually caught fire. The firefighters on duty scrambled to their trucks and raced out of the building, only to turn around and realize they had to go back to their own building.

When I arrived home that afternoon, the building was in fire, and the news stations were on the scene. I turned and ran two blocks up the street and into an insurance office, where an old classmate of mine was working.

"What can I do for you, Kenny?"

"I need some fire insurance, quick!"

Let me back up and say I had hundreds - no, thousands! - of dollars in stereo equipment and other electronics in my room. I had no insurance on any of it, and if our apartment burned, it would all be gone. My old classmate pulled out some paperwork, and we were running the numbers when his boss came in.

"Kenny wants to take our a fire insurance policy," my old friend said.

The manager knew exactly who I was and where I lived. He put a stop to that right away. He even had the audacity to label me "high risk." Me!

Jim Cornette

Kenny's apartment was literally the highest point in Oldham County, which made it ideal for trying to get TV signals from far away. Kenny installed an antenna on the chimney of the firehouse illegally. One day while he was out front, the wind blew and ripped that antenna right off the chimney. It flew like a javelin into the street and came a few feet away from impaling a pedestrian!

The antenna served an important purpose. It was part of our never ending pursuit of more wrestling. Back then we didn't have cable, so we relied on the antenna to bring in wrestling locally and beyond. Sun spots played a key role in how far those antenna signals could travel, and during the summer of 1978 we were able to find 114 stations that carried either wrestling or Underdog. At one point we even got channel 3 out of Denver, Colorado.

Kenny

Some times we had to go up on the roof to get a good signal. I had a battery operated TV that enabled us to roam freely in search of the best reception. One time we were up on the roof trying to watch Angelo Poffo's International Championship Wrestling from Lexington. We kept moving the TV back and forth across the rooftops trying to get a good signal. Someone must have spotted us because they called the police on us. Two cop cars pulled up in front of the house, and four cops got out with their guns drawn. About that time, the train came through, blocking their view of us. I slipped in the window and went down to the street to talk to the police and explain what was happening. I'm not sure they believed us. Matter of fact I'm not sure they believed we were the same guys they saw on the roof.

Jim Cornette

As if we hadn't caused enough trouble that night, we decided to go out zombie walking later that night. We staggered down the road with our track suit jackets zipped up over our faces, moaning and groaning like a couple of zombies. We ended up in front of a funeral home, bumping and stumbling around doing our zombie act. About that time, two more cops arrived, ordering the zombies to pull over.

"What's the matter, officer?" said Kenny, who pretty much knew every cop in Oldham County.

"We got a report of a couple assholes walking around like zombies in front of a funeral home," said the cop. He advised us to zombie walk our way home, which we did.

Kenny

Jim and I were both obsessed with electronics. We always wanted to have the best and newest gear, whether it was turntables, tape decks, or later on, VCR's. Jim got the first VCR, a VHS player. I still say the greatest rib he ever played on me was convincing me to buy a Betamax player.

There used to be a place on Shelbyville Road called Hi-Fi Buys. We were always out for a deal, and we knew cash spoke loudly. One day we walked in with brown bags stuffed with cash, about $900 each. We drew dollar signs on the bag and marched in saying, "We want a deal!" Dave Nakdimen, who was then the troubleshooter for Wave 3 news, was in the store. He laughed at us and told us it probably wasn't a good idea to walk into a store with bags of money like that.

"Oh no?" I said. "You're supposed to be the money expert. We're just a couple of kids. And we got the better deal!"

Dave Nakdimen laughed. "You're right, kid, you did."

Jim and I bought our own electronic equipment, but we had an arrangement when it came to music. When one of us bought an album, the other would pay "reproduction rights," usually just under half the cost of the album, to copy it off the other guy.

Jim Cornette

Kenny had to have surgery at Jewish Hospital one time. There was a girl we knew from the Gardens who lived in New Albany. She rode her bike across the bridge to visit Kenny every day while he was in the hospital.

When Kenny got out, he wanted to go see this girl to "repay her for her kindness." He convinced me to drive him over there to her house. When I got there, I found out that I was expected to wait in the living room while he spent time with her in the bedroom. I was also told I was going to have to sit in the dark so the girl's father would not see a light on and think anything was going on!

There I was, sitting in the dark in a strange house, watching television. I went into the kitchen to find some food, and to my horror, I saw bugs. Lots of bugs. I absolutely HATE bugs, and I knew from the quantity of bugs I found in the kitchen, this house was infested.

I went back to the living room and sat down on the edge of the couch, unable to relax because I knew there were bug everywhere. I finally couldn't take it any more. I got up and flipped on the light. Soon as I did, Kenny came marching down the hall. He gives me this Oliver Hardy look of indignation and shuts off the light.

The longer I sat in the dark, the more crazed I became. I started stomping my feet and slapping my legs. Kenny, who had no idea why I was doing what I was doing, yelled at me and told me I was killing the mood. I didn't care! I wanted to get out of the damn house and away from the bugs.

24

On the way home that night, Kenny lit into me for ruining his night. I explained to him why I was going to crazy, stomping my feet and slapping my legs. I never wanted to cross that bridge into Indiana again, let alone go to that girl's house. As we crossed back into Kentucky, I wished aloud that we could take a sledgehammer and destroy that bridge completely.

Kenny

My sister Janice was always inviting shady characters over to the house, especially when no one was around. Jimmy and I finally decided we would do something about it before one of them decided to get into my room. We got our buddy Adrian Reynolds to help us out.

We announced that we were heading to Showcase Cinemas in Louisville and would be back late. We drove down the street, parked in the Kroger parking lot, and walked back to the house with baseball bats.

The plan was for Jimmy and I to enter the front door to scare these boys off. We told Adrian to go around back to herd any strays back into the house. We told him to chase them but not to hit them. Adrian remembered everything he was told - except that last part. He had to get at least two or three shots in on each of those guys before they could scramble back inside the house. We cut promos on Janice's boyfriends and warned them never to come around the house again.

Adrian was over at the house another time when he fell asleep in my room. Jimmy and I decided to leave him there while we went to get lunch. If we woke him up, one of us would end up having to pay for Adrian.

When we came back, Adrian was still asleep. We decided to throw frisbee out front. Jimmy sent one sailing over my head. I missed it and ended up crashing into the front door, breaking the pane glass window. I wasn't hurt, but I was scared, knowing that someone would have to pay for the window. Rather than stick around and take the blame, we hopped in the car and drove off.

We came back a short while later and "discovered" the broken window. We put on quite a performance as two teens completely innocent of the crime. We walked in the house and found Adrian finally awake. "Did you see what happened?"

"Yes, yes, I saw it!" said Adrian nervously. "There were two guys, big guys. They smashed your window. I tried to chase them down, but they got away from me."

Jim and I never told Adrian the truth. Best as we could figure, the poor guy woke up, saw the broken glass, and figured he better come up with a story so he wouldn't be blamed.

Years later, Adrian went to prison, where he was beaten to death. When President Bill Clinton gave his speech about curbing violence in prisons, he held a photo of one of the many men who fall victim to such violence every year. It was our dear friend, Adrian Reynolds.

Jim Cornette

When we weren't talking wrestling, we sometimes performed little social experiments. Once we went down to the mall - now known as Oxmoor

Mall - and staged a fight in the parking lot. We beat the hell out of each other in that parking lot in full view of at least fifty people. I pretended to take a tire iron to the eye. I was screaming, "My eye, Rison, my eye!" as he threw me into the trunk of the car. He pulled out and drove off. No one called the cops.

We did something similar on main street in LaGrange all the time. Around midnight, one of us would go out and sit on a bench along side the road. The other would hide in the bushes nearby. When a car came along, the guy in the bushes would leap out, clock the guy on the bench in the head, take his wallet, and run back to the bushes. No one ever stopped to help. In fact most people sped up when they saw it happen.

The last time we did this, in 1979, I was the guy on the bench. I'm pretty sure Kenny didn't return my wallet that time!

Kenny

One night at Louisville Gardens, Jimmy gave me a tip. It was when he was taking photos, so he had access to backstage. He came up to me and told me that Bill Dundee would be going over Nelson Royals that night to win the NWA World Junior Heavyweight Championship.

Title changes never happened at the Gardens. Never, never, never! I knew I had a sure thing on my hands. I went around the Gardens finding every mark I knew to take me up on the bet that Dundee would win the title. By the time the match rolled around, I had $150 in bets.

Did I mention already that titles never changed hands at Louisville Gardens?

Royals pinned Dundee, one, two, three. Royals retained the title. Jim turned to me and shrugged - as if he didn't know. I did the only thing I knew to do. I took a door I had never used, the side door, and got out of the arena!

Jim Cornette

Any hopes that Kenny had of one day being a wrestler were dispelled thanks to his time in the KWA - the Kentucky Wrestling Alliance. Don't look it up on Google; you won't find it. The KWA was our own little promotion that we ran from time to time, usually in the Oldham County boys locker room.

Kenny had a few memorable matches in the KWA, one being a match with his brother Timmy John. Timmy John watched almost as much wrestling as we did. Kenny didn't bother to discuss the match beforehand with Timmy John because he figured he knew what to do. I was the referee. Kenny was calling the shots in the match, and he told Timmy John to push him against a wall and hit him.

Well, Timmy John wasn't "smart" like the two of us. Timmy John hit Kenny in the face with everything he had! It sounded like someone hitting a watermelon with a sledgehammer as Kenny's head bounced off Timmy John's fist and off the brick wall behind him.

Lucky for Kenny, he knew every locker in that locker room, and he knew where he could get his hands on one of those giant aerosol Right Guard cans. I turned my back, pretending to be distracted while Kenny gave Timmy John a shot to the head with that metal can. I delivered a quick count and the match ended.

Another time, Kenny decided to hit his opponent in the mouth as hard as he could with his forearm. The kid went down hard, knocked out cold.

I stood over the kid and shook my head. "What the hell were you thinking, Kenny? You smashed his teeth in!"

The unconscious kid's brother leaned over to take a look. "Naw, that's how his teeth always looked!"

Kenny

I had a buddy at Oldham County, Mike Heilman, who fancied himself to be the Sam Bass to my Jerry Lawler. One time the two of us ran afoul of Brian Blair and Steve Rogers, the school's top two football players. The football players wanted to fight after school behind the buses. Heilman and I agreed to fight, but we decided to choose a different venue - the school halls.

We caught Blair and Rogers right after class. Right away, Rogers and Heilman backed out of the fight, leaving me to pummel Blair alone. It didn't take long for the coaches and the principal to swarm us.

"Break it up, Muhammed Ali," said the principal.

"Muhammed Ali??" said Heilman. "Hell no, that's Jerry 'The King' Lawler!"

They took us down to the office to mete out justice. "What's it gonna be, boys?" the principal asked. "Licks or suspension?"

"Well, sir," I said. "You ain't touching me, and I could use a vacation. I'll take suspension."

"If I'm suspended, I'm off the football team," said Blair. "I'll take licks."

"Can I watch?" I said.

Blair took his licks in the office, but he got kicked off the team anyway. By the time I returned to school, I was a legend.

Being the Lawler fan I was, I often signed my papers "King Rison," looping the words together like Jerry did. One day one of my teachers asked me, "Kenny what are you the king of?"

"Wrestling!" I said.

"We'll see about that," she said.

I guess I showed her!

Looking back on those days, I have great fondness for the memories made in high school and at home, but it was never easy. We didn't have money like my rich friend Jim Cornette, and it was always a struggle to make ends meet. But I made a vow that one day, things would be different. I told my mother I was going to provide for her and our family. I would enter the wrestling business. I would make millions, and we would never want for anything again!

Terry Garvin Simms

You know, I equate Kenny Bolin with Jim Cornette. They're both Kentucky boy through and through, just like me. There's always been some sort of feud between Cornette and Bolin, but Bolin has always had a great mind for the business. I don't think Jimmy gives Kenny enough credit for the things he has done.

Kenny and Jimmy couldn't have been any more different. Jimmy was a mama's boy. His mother loved him, took him wherever he wanted, and got him whatever he needed. Kenny had to scrap and scrape for everything he got. When Jimmy got into the business, it was due in part to his mom's friendship with Teeny Jarrett, who really ran the show in Louisville for her son Jerry. He had been taking photos for the wrestlers for years, and when they needed a manager, Jerry Jarrett figured he'd give Jimmy a shot.

I have no doubt that Kenny could have made it just as well as Jimmy. He has a gift on the mic, and he always has a game plan. I don't know whether he would have applied himself and committed to life on the road like we lived, but if he had, he would have gone far. If there's was a Hall of Fame for Kentucky rasslers, they'd both belong in it. No question.

BISCUITS AND GRAVY, OR HOW I KNEW JIMMY WAS GOING TO BE A TOP PROMOTER

I mentioned earlier that I had a brother named Timmy John. Timmy John, also known as Biscuits and Gravy, also known as The Man With A Thousand Nicknames, did not grow up in the same house with me. We shared the same biological mother, but not the same father. Shocking, given what I've already told you about Ma Bolin, but true!

Ma Bolin struggled with as many kids as she had, so Timmy John was adopted by one of my aunts and uncles. My aunt was a waitress who worked for a well-to-do Kentucky couple you may have heard of: Claudia and Colonel Harland Sanders.

Colonel Sanders is one of the great success stories of the 20th century. Sanders was born in 1890 not in Kentucky, but across the river in Henryville, Indiana. He held a number of jobs in his early years, from a street car conductor to an attorney. Sanders lost his license to practice law when he got into a brawl with someone in the courtroom. That's my kind of lawyer, if you ask me!

Eventually, Sanders went into the restaurant business. He perfected a secret spice recipe and a quick method for cooking fried chicken that, in time, made him a millionaire. Today, the Colonel with his white hair, white beard, black string tie, and white suit are still the face of KFC.

Timmy John's adopted parents were about as poor as we were. The only reason they were worse off was because Timmy John didn't have my keen sense for managing money. Colonel Sanders really liked Timmy John's mom, and he looked out for her. For a long time, my brother actually lived in the same home as Colonel Sanders. The Colonel and Claudia helped raise my brother, and the Colonel whipped my brother on more than one occasion when he needed it. Hand to God!

The Colonel had a cane that was gifted to him by an Arab sheik. One day, the Colonel's cane went missing, and the police were called out to help look. The cane was incredibly valuable, decorated with all sorts of jewels and stones. The Colonel offered a reward to whomever might find the cane.

Timmy John and his family joined in the search, and it was Timmy John who spotted the cane in the Colonel's garden. Timmy John brought it to the attention of one of the policemen. Wouldn't you know it, that dirty cop grabbed the cane, raced into the house, and tried to take credit for the find!

Luckily, Timmy John had a witness he never knew was watching. Claudia Sanders saw the whole thing happen out in the garden, and right in front of the policeman and the Colonel, she let it be known that the little boy staying with the Colonel and his wife was the one who found the cane.

"Come on over, son," said the Colonel. "Come get your reward."

The Colonel handed a reward to my brother in cold, hard cash, but before young Timmy John could pocket the money, his mother stepped in.

"Timmy John, Colonel Sanders and his wife have been too good to us. Don't you think you should give that reward back, to thank him for all the good things he's done for us?"

That's right, that cruel, cold-hearted woman made my brother give back the money.

Rico Costantino

Kenny invited me over to his house one day when his brother was in for a visit. We were sitting in the living room talking when all of a sudden, Kenny's brother takes off his socks and shoes. That was bad enough, but then this guy starts to clip his toe nails! He was clipping his toe nails on the King's coffee table. I tried to ignore it, but he kept at it, clipping and dropping, clipping and dropping. I finally had enough and yelled at him. "What the fuck are you doing??" Kenny looked over and said, "What the fuck, Timmy John??"

Kenny Bolin

Spending time with my brother was always an experience, especially as I got older. Timmy John wasn't the wrestling fan that Jimmy and I were, but he dabbled a bit in a different type of fighting sport.

One night, the three of us were at Druthers Restaurant, trying to figure out what to do. Almost innocently, my brother made mention that he knew a place that had cockfighting going on that night. Jimmy and I had never been to a cockfight, and since wrestling wouldn't be on TV anywhere for several hours, we decided to check it out.

We drove out to Lockport, Kentucky, to a giant barn. No sooner did we spot it, Jimmy shouted out, "That must be where they have the cockfights!" Master of the obvious, that boy.

We went inside and discovered a sea of humanity and poultry. People were elbow to elbow in that joint, and the evening's entertainment was on display. Cock trainers had their birds out for public viewing so that the fans could check out the competitors before placing their bets.

Right away, I figured Timmy John had been here before. He knew way too many people, and I got the feeling Timmy John might have owned a cock or two himself.

Jim, on the other hand, seemed at first like a man out of his element. Walking inside, he turned to my brother and I and asked, "What are all these chickens doing here?"

A man approached and asked if we had a cock to enter for the fights. We said no, and he asked if we wanted to place our bets. Jim was all in. Next thing I knew, he was going from cock to cock. He examined them, held them, felt them. In the hour before they started the fights, Jim probably laid his hands on every cock in that barn!

Now here's how I knew that night that Jimmy had a future in promotion. Like I said, Jim gave every cock he saw a good, hard look. After checking and feeling all those cocks, Jim placed a few bets. He won the first match. He won the second. He won the third. Jim was on a roll, winning bet after bet. You wouldn't know it was his first time the way he handled all those cocks!

Truth be told, Jim might have won even more money. After winning several fights in a row, he disappeared. After being gone about twenty minutes, Jim returned. "Where were you?" I asked.

"I was in the bathroom," he said. "One of the trainers said he had a prized cock he wanted to show me."

Thirteen fights later, we went out to the car to head home. Jimmy won eleven of those thirteen fights, a stunning demonstration of his natural gift for scouting talent.

"Hey, Kenny?" he said as we pulled onto the main road. "I think those folks might have been racists."

"No shit," I said. "This is Lockport, Kentucky. Of course they're all racists!"

"No, Kenny," he said. "That's not the reason. When we were in that barn I looked everywhere, and I didn't see a single black cock!"

BOLIN SERVICES, ZERO YEAR

Many people know about my years in the wrestling business and the incredible work I did transforming men like John Cena into superstars. Little is known about my early career, about Bolin Services pre-wrestling.

My earliest years can best be described as a series of starts and stops. My first job was at a place called Burger Queen. I went to work for them in 1976, partly because they needed help, but mainly because they wanted King Bolin on their softball team. The season lasted three months, and sadly, so did my employment with Burger Queen.

Like a superstar athlete, I was picked up in the summer of 1977 by Long John Silvers, who wanted me on their softball team. For some inexplicable reason, they also cut me from the restaurant staff as soon as the season ended.

I was then hired by Mallory Taylor Hospital, who did not have a softball team. I worked there for about two years and then moved on to Kroger's.

As you might expect, I always had a thing or two going on the side in addition to my day jobs. The King has always been on the lookout for an opportunity, and at once point in my pre-wrestling days, I established myself as a leading expert on fraud and fraud prevention.

For those who were not around in the 1980s and 90s, our country did not have the many safeguards we now enjoy against theft and general dishonesty. Many states did not put photos on driver's licenses. Credit cards were not run electronically at the register, but copied on two part receipt paper. In short it was the wild, wild west, and I took it upon myself to play sheriff in this western drama.

My work in fraud prevention began when I was working for both Kroger and another grocery store, GT&Y. As a clerk at GT&Y, I was entrusted with one of the price guns used to label store merchandise. One day I accidentally took the price gun home with me. When I discovered my error, it made me realize how easy it would be for anyone, not just me, to sneak a price gun from the store.

I was curious just how far one could take such an action, so the following day, I went into work early. I began marking discounted prices on various items in the store. I gathered these items into a basket and took them to the register. To my shock and dismay, the clerk, my co-worker, rang the items up at the phony prices without so much as batting an eye.

Clearly, I was on to something.

I continued my studies at GT&Y for some time, and I soon discovered that every item in the story was vulnerable. I even discounted a chainsaw down from $195 to $65 at the behest of my brother Timmy John. I was very proud of this discovery, but I knew this was just the tip of the iceberg.

It was around this time that my employment with Kroger came to an abrupt end. My manager David King became angry with me one day when I refused to stay over. I explained to the man that I had a second job, as he well knew, and I was needed at GT&Y. I also had some more pricing research to do that required me to be at the job a little early.

Things came to a head one day when this Mr. King accused me of stealing a sixty-nine cent sausage biscuit. I had picked up two sausage biscuits to eat on my break, but by the time I reached the register, one of the two was already gone. The cashier only rang me up for one, and when Mr. King found out, he read me the riot act. The dumbass called me a fat, lazy bastard, and I punched him in the face.

Had I kept my cool, I might have been able to come out on top against that bastard. Keith Koebel, the union steward, was and is a good friend and was ready to come to my defense. But after I took a swing at the boss, it was all over for me.

I felt vindicated some time later when I learned that David King was himself fired for stealing from Kroger. King went a little further than the crime he accused me of committing, embezzling thousands in cash and merchandise from the deli and catering departments.

Long story short, I found myself with more free time for this research project, I jumped in with both feet.

Jim Cornette

Kenny had his "research" down to a science. Not only did he have a price gun, he had a shrink wrap machine. Don't ask me how he got his hands on that. He probably stole that too.

Kenny

After procuring a shrink wrap machine, I decided to look into the video game market. Video games were just beginning to hit their stride, and where there was money, I suspected there would soon be thieves taking advantage.

It did not take long for me to discover just how wily crooks could make a quick cash cow of video games. Step one, the perpetrator would hit up video rental stores that rented games and getting hold of the discarded video game boxes.

Step two, the perpetrators filled the empty boxes with something that gave the box the feel of a video game. After trying several options, I learned that a Betamax video tape was the perfect size and weight. It also sounded like a game cartridge, in case a suspicious clerk were to shake the box.

Step three was to seal the box with the shrink wrap machine. Having done so, one only had to take the re-sealed video game box back to the store to "return" the game. A clever man could return several at a time, and the store would refund the money without question. Stores did not require receipts back then, another hole I found in their system, so there was no safeguard against this sort of dishonest.

I ran a number of studies on video game returns in Kentucky, but after a time, I decided to take my experiment on the road. I packed up the family and we moved to Florida, where I and a few relatives ran a full blown sting operation to test my theories on video game theft. Were we successful? I should say so. I arrived in Florida with $200 in my pocket. I left with $3000 and a truck full of cigarettes that I would sell to Ma Bolin and her friends.

While in Florida I expanded my independent research. An old roommate of mine whom we will call George Namewitheld left a book of checks behind after leaving my place. I decided to test and see how easy it would be to used George's checks. Imagine my dismay when retailers began taking these checks with no hesitation at all. Check after check went out, and not once did anyone ask for identification of anything.

By random chance, my research expanded once again to credit cards. One day while taking my son the Prince to Chuck E. Cheese with some other relatives, my tire blew out. As we were walking the road to the restaurant, my niece spotted a twenty dollar bill. She then spotted a ten, a five, another twenty, and another ten.

Next, she spotted a brand new Discover card. She discovered a Chevron card, and several more cards. Someone had had a fight in the car and, in a moment of rage, chucked their wallet out the window. It was exactly the sort of foolish action that leads to credit card fraud, as I was about to prove.

I used the cards to buy dinner at Chuck E. Cheese, gas, and tires. No one batted an eye, no one raised a red flag. I continued my experiment with the credit card another two years.

Finally, the study came to an end. I walked into the gas station to pay for my gas and spotted an electronic credit card reader. I knew then that all my hard work had paid off. Stores were finally getting wise to the schemes and scams that had no doubt cost them thousands of dollars. Satisfied that all my hard work had not been in vain, I disposed of the card and left the independent consulting business.

Today, such wicked schemes are simply not possible. Driver's licenses require photos. Credit cards are all run on the spot. Stores require receipts for returns. Credit card companies have flags built into their software to detect trends and possible fraud violations.

I can't take credit for all these advances. I'm just one man, and while I spent a great deal of my time researching different ways people could cheat the system, I spent very little time, if any, reporting my findings back to those who would benefit most, the retailers. Nevertheless, I can't help but feel a swell of pride whenever I hear someone ask to see an ID.

I BECOME A FRIEND TO THE GREAT, THE NEAR GREAT, AND THE PISS BOYS

Even before I established myself in the wrestling business (thanks in no part to certain so-called friends of mine), I was making friends and influencing people. One of the first men to recognize the value of Mr. Kenny Bolin was promoter Dennis Corralluzzo.

Jim Cornette
Corralluzzo was an insurance salesman from Woodbury, New Jersey. He was a big wrestling fan who decided to become a promoter. At a time when most territories were failing, Corralluzzo opened and ran a thriving promotion in the North East. Corralluzzo even served as president of what was left of the NWA. He was Tony Soprano without the murders - at least I think so.

Kenny
I was living in Nashville when I got a call from Corralluzzo. He asked me to rent a rental car and drive to Memphis so I could give him a ride back, all for a nice fee. I rented the car and drove to Memphis as requested.

I became one of Corralluzzo's most trusted friends, so much so that one day, Corralluzzo sent me on a shopping trip. "You're going shopping, Kenny," he told me. "I want you to go shopping and get some new clothes for yourself."

"For me?"

"Yes," said Corralluzzo. "Get some stuff for you and some stuff for the Prince. All I ask is that you get me a new camera, and maybe a new sweater for my wife."

Corralluzzo reached into his pocket and handed me two brand new credit cards, each with a $5000 limit. "You've got ten hours. Go spend these on yourself, your son, my wife, and a camera. And get some new clothes for the Piss Boys."

The Piss Boys, as he called them, were two fellas Corralluzzo took with him as his personal servants. The nickname came from Mel Brooks' *History of the World Part One.* The boys carried Corralluzzo's bags, ran errands, and did other odd jobs. They even dressed alike.

"Anything else you need, Kenny?" Corralluzzo asked me.

"Yes, sir," I said. "I could use a video camera for my wedding video business."

"Get one," said Corralluzzo. He handed me his Pennsylvania driver's license - which did NOT have a photo on it - and told me to present it as my ID. Corralluzzo and I had similar signatures, so I knew this would be a walk in the park.

Jim Cornette

Ah yes, the wedding photography business. If memory serves me right, I invested a couple thousand dollars in that business. Either that, or his video yearbook business. I don't remember which one it was, but I know he didn't do many weddings or yearbooks. He also never paid me back for the

44

thousands of dollars in editing equipment I bought for him.

Kenny

Ten hours later the Piss Boys and I carried all of our shopping bags back to Corralluzzo's hotel room. I had purchased a $1300 video camera, cameras for everyone, new clothes for me and the Piss Boys, and clothes for Corralluzzo's wife. I also bought a Philadelphia Eagles shirt and an Underdog toy for my son Chris. Corralluzzo insisted I give them to my son from his God-Uncle Dennis.

A few months later, the government showed up at Corralluzzo's house with a warrant. They searched his house and found the camera, the clothes, and a number of other things that were purchased with his "stolen" cards. I guess no one was interested in the things purchased for me or the Piss Boys because we never received a visit.

Another stylin' and profilin' acquaintance of mine was none other than Ric Flair. I had the good fortune to meet and get to know Flair on several occasions when my buddy Jim graciously allowed me to tag along with him and the Midnight Express. One night in Cincinnati, February of 1986 to be exact, Flair made a bet with me. He knew I was a Louisville fan, and he offered a bet. "If North Carolina faces Louisville in the NCAA tournament, North Carolina will win. I'll even give you 10 to 1 odds."

"Just to be clear," I said, "If I bet you $100, and Louisville wins, you'll pay me $1000?" Flair said yes, and we shook on the bet.

Later that night I had a hair-raising experience thanks to Jimmy's Midnight Express associate,

Dennis Condry. I had purchased a brand new Nissan Pulsar. It was a sweet car, but it was a manual, and yours truly was never that skilled behind the wheel of a manual. I made it to Cincinnati okay, but I asked if someone else would mind driving back to the Drawbridge Inn, where everyone was staying.

Condry assured me he knew how to drive a stick. That might have been true, but that doesn't mean he could drive it well. And of course Cornette and Condry's tag partner Bobby Eaton didn't feel the need to smarten me up to that fact. Jim and Bobby rode in the back while I rode shotgun. Condry was flying through the streets of Northern Kentucky, whipping around cars and running red lights like he was driving the Indy 500.

The car survived the ride that night, as did we, but I know for a fact that clutch gave out much faster than normal.

Jim Cornette

When the Midnight Express and I were working in Texas, we had to make a regular trip to Corpus Christi. It was a small town with a bad pay off, but it was the price we paid to work in Dallas. One night Condry got behind the wheel of my car and drove us from Corpus Christi to Dallas. It was a straight shot across Texas, and Condry did 115 miles an hour all the way.

As we got closer to Dallas, the engine clanked and started to make a terrible sound. Eaton leaned forward and asked what that noise was. "I'll fix it," said Condry. He reached over and turned up the radio. "There, fixed."

Turns out a rod had come loose in the engine. Condry of course knew a shade tree mechanic, and $800 later, he got the car running again.

Dennis Condry could drive any car ever made… straight into the ground.

Kenny

So back to my good friend Ric Flair. As I said, it was February of 1986, and if you know college basketball, you know my Louisville Cardinals won their second championship that year. The Cardinals did meet the Tar Heels in the tournament, and they won by 23 points.

I was in Atlanta when I caught up to Flair and asked him to pay up. Flair responded by grabbing me with his taped hands and dragging me into the heel locker room.

Jim Cornette

When I saw Flair drag Kenny into the heel locker room, I wasn't worried about him getting stretched. I was worried about him getting cut. Flair had all his fingers taped, and under one of those fingers was the razor blade he used to cut himself every night in the ring.

I don't know how Kenny avoided getting cut, but Flair didn't hurt him. And thanks to Bobby Eaton, Kenny collected on his bet.

Kenny

"Just so you know," Ric Flair said, counting hundred dollar bills out of his wallet, "This is my dinner money tonight."

"Just so you know," I said. "This is my rent for the next three months."

Ric bitched about paying up, but in truth, Ric was a man who loved to spend money. It wasn't uncommon for Ric to pick up the tab for everyone in the restaurant when he went out to dinner. Not just his table, mind you, I mean the whole restaurant. Ric should have hung out with me more. I would have taught him how he could have covered himself, his guests, and anyone else he wanted without spending a dime, but we'll get into how I manage all that later.

THE BALLAD OF THE DOUBLE YOUR MONEY BACK GUARANTEE

So much has been said and spoken about a certain part of my past involving myself and a regional grocery chain, I didn't even think it worthy of inclusion in this book. The story has been told by many people, myself included, on podcasts and at wrestling gatherings. It is only by popular demand that I chose to put down in writing the full story of what happened.

It all began one day when I went to my local grocery store to purchase food for a dinner I was hosting. Some old friends were coming over, and I wanted to do something special. The King has always enjoyed putting on a feast for friends and followers, as any fan, wrestler, and Beets by Bolin customer who has ever joined me at the Golden Corral can attest. I went to the very fine meat counter and selected a large side of beef, more than I needed for the occasion but plenty big to save some back for another time. On arriving home, I split the meat, putting half in the freezer and preparing the other half for our meal.

Dinner was fine, but during the main course, one of my guests noticed a bit of gristle in his meat that made it unappetizing. Another guest found gristle as well, and the discovery made the meal a minor disappointment. When I mentioned the name of the store where I purchased the meat – a name I will withhold, so as to keep from defaming their good name – I was reminded that the store had a promotional campaign specifically for their meat products. "If you are not completely satisfied, return the unused portion, and we will give you double your money back."

I returned the meat from dinner as instructed. With no questions asked, the grocery store took the meat back and gave me double my money in return. I came home two hundred dollars ahead and feeling good. It certainly put me in the frame of mind to become a loyal customer to this particular chain, which was the purpose of the campaign, right?

In all the excitement of getting my money back and discovering a company that was truly as good as their word, I had forgotten one thing: the second half of the meat was still sitting in the freezer! Knowing that the first half of the meat was full of gristle, I had no desire to cook this half, so I packed it up and returned it.

Did I go to a different store to return the rest of the meat? Yes I did. Was it my intent to go to a different store and try to get quadruple my money back? No. I simply chose the location most convenient to me at that time. Happy to say the folks in the second store were just as friendly and pleased to give me double my money back.

In the following weeks and months I became one of the most loyal customers this grocer had ever known. I would shop the meat counter for the biggest and priciest cuts of meat, take them home, and prepare them for my dear friends and neighbors. When a piece of meat turned out to be less than promised, I returned it. Some might say I was taking advantage of the system, particularly those occasions where I would forget half the meat was in the freezer and return it to a second store. I never saw it that way. My friendly neighborhood meat counter wanted my business. I gave it to them, and when they did not give me the quality product I expected from their brand, they honored their double your money pledge.

It was only when my mother, dear old Ma Bolin, decided to get in on the action that my loyalty as a meat customer came to an end. Ma purchased a rather large side of beef just as I did. Ma halved it, cooked it, found some gristle, and returned that half to the store to get double her money.

Later that day, I took Ma to a second store to return the second half of the meat. She came out of the store moments later with no meat and no money. Tears were streaming down her face.

"What happened, Ma?" I said.

"Kenny, the manager on duty was at the other store," said Ma. "He recognized me, and he said if I ever tried to return meat again, he'd call the cops on me!"

I couldn't believe it. How greedy of that corporate puppet to threaten my mother, dear old Ma Bolin, with jail! And all because of a customer satisfaction campaign they themselves created.

I can't say for sure whether Ma was the reason, but soon after, the double your money back pledge was rescinded. All good things must come to an end, I suppose. It's just a shame some power-tripping meat cutter decided to go Dirty Harry on my mother before it did.

Jim Cornette

I woke up one morning to the sound of someone pounding on my front door. I put on my robe and slippers and made my way out front to discover the Louisville Metro Police Department waiting for me with a pair of meat cutters from Kroger. They had an arrest warrant with my name on it stating that I had tried to rip the good people of Kroger off over some meat.

Thankfully, the meat cutters were there to tell the police, "No, this is not the fat bastard who tried to rip us off." They checked my ID, asked a few questions about where I was the day before, and went away.

Come to find out when Kroger got wise to his little scam, the suspect had given his name as "Jim Cornette" before ducking out of the store. I knew right away who was responsible.

Kenny

No story has haunted me to the extent this little episode of my life has. When Jim Cornette revealed the story to my dear friend and mentor Jerry Jarrett, it crushed him. Thanks to the spin Jimmy put on the tale, Jarrett saw me as a crook and a con artist.

I never thought of my actions as anything wrong. I was a husband and a father struggling to make ends meet and put food on the table. Yes, the grocery store in question had recently terminated my employment. Yes, that played some part in my decision to run the meat operation like I did. But what loving father wouldn't do everything he could to provide for his beloved wife and children?

PAPA JOHN AND THE WORLD'S GREATEST SALESMAN

Eventually, I gave up the undercover work for good and decided to rejoin the 9 to 5 work force. Not wanting to return to the hellish world of retail, I found myself entering the then burgeoning field of telemarketing. It was there I discovered I truly had a gift for gab and a silver tongue. I also learned a few other skills that have served me well.

I was working for Humana, one of Louisville's largest employers, when I first learned the art of the barter. One day I stopped at a Papa John's to grab a pizza. At that time, Papa John's was still a small, fledgling pizza company, not the juggernaut it has now become. Papa John himself was working behind the counter, and he recognized me as being a Humana employee. Papa John himself then asked me a question that would change my life.

"How would you like to earn two free pizzas a week?" he asked.

"What would I have to do to get them?" I replied.

"How many floors do you have access to in your office building?" he asked.

"Well, Papa John," I said, "I can get on just about any floor you want."

"How about downtown?" he said, referring to the giant corporate headquarters that graces the Louisville skyline. "Can you get into that building as well?"

"Yes, sir," I said.

"If you can get fliers on every floor for me when I have them, I'll give you two pizzas a week."

We shook hands, and I told my new friend, "You got yourself a deal, Papa Johns."

Papa John's a smart businessman, and in no time at all, our little barter deal paid off. Papa John told me himself a large pizza, at that time, cost him only $3 to make. He was paying $6 a week for a marketing distribution deal that was making him big bucks. It was so successful, I managed to negotiate an increase to four pizzas a week.

Now as you might expect, eating all that pizza makes a man a little sick of eating pizza, but rather than turn down my four pizzas a week, I started turning around and selling them to my co-workers by the slice. I had my pizzas delivered to work at Humana, and people were lining up to buy a slice off the King.

People who say I never pay for a meal and always eat free are misinformed at best and ignorant at worst. It's called the barter system, and it still works. Thank you, Papa John, for sharing it with me.

I earned numerous awards at Humana as a top salesman, and not just for selling pizza. I was damn good at selling insurance as well. But my greatest sales job was with a company called Royal Prestige, makers and marketers of fine China and cookware.

I went to work for Royal Prestige right after my dismissal from Kroger's. My sister found the ad in the paper, and I went down for an interview. I showed up in a blue seersucker suit with a pink shirt and tie, an ensemble I had received as a gift from Jim when I helped him move to Louisiana.

I was a total fish out of water in that office with that suit on, but as fate would have it, they saw potential in me. "Anybody who would come in here dressed like that, who has a way with words like you, is bound to be a great salesman."

So impressed were these fine gentlemen, they began to spell out the challenges of the job on the spot. "We normally wait until two weeks into training before we even tell you what our product costs," they said. "A full set can run as much as $2500."

"What's the commission?" I asked.

"Ten percent," they said.

I shook my head. "That seems a little low. I think we can do better."

"Prove yourself, and we'll see what we can do," they said. We shook hands, and I became the newest sales rep for Royal Prestige.

Royal Prestige sold door to door, the old fashioned way. Early on, I found it a struggle to ramp up sales. I'd set appointments to meet with people in their homes, and about fifty percent would cancel on me. A few years in, that number dropped to two percent. I became the top salesman in the company in no time, and that ten percent commission began to climb rapidly. Ten became twelve, and twelve became fifteen.

One day I found myself in Henryville, Indiana, about twenty miles north of Louisville. I got there only to find out that my appointment had canceled. I was still living in LaGrange at the time, and I didn't want to drive back empty-handed.

I went into a convenience store and spotted a young man working the counter. "Son," I said, "How would you like to make some money today?"

"Sure thing, mister," he said.

I told him who I was and what I was selling and how my appointment had canceled. Then I asked him, "Would you happen to know any young ladies of marrying age who might be looking to move out and will be in need of some fine cookware?"

"Are you kidding?" he said. "I know a bunch of girls, fresh out of high school. If they're not already engaged, they will be. This is the country. We all get married young."

"Excellent," I said. "And what would you want in return? For every young lady you hook me up with who buys, what would be fair compensation?"

"How about a case of beer?" he said.

I said, "That sounds fine."

My young friend was on the phone in minutes talking to one girl after another. He was giving them the sales pitch, pre-selling the merchandise for me as he set up one appointment after another. Over the next eight days, I sold sixteen sets of cookware or China. Some applied for credit. Some paid cash. Cash meant instant commission, my favorite kind of sale.

By the time I was done, I sold forty sets of cookware in Henryville. That little town became my go-to when sales were slow, and I always made money any time I returned.

The more I sold, the more Royal Prestige pressed me to sell. They wanted me out there as much as possible, but they made a mistake. They labeled me as an independent contractor. To me, independent contractor meant I worked for myself. I set my own hours, and I didn't answer to the higher ups who wanted me to keep office hours and sell round the clock.

I was 24 years old, loaded with cash, and worn out, so I went to Florida with my grandma. I didn't tell anyone where I was going, not even my Mom. We were there three months before anyone knew where I was.

I didn't spent the whole time goofing off. When my bosses finally got me on the phone, I informed them of the nine cash sales I had made. You'd think that would make them happy, but they only wanted me to sell, sell, and sell some more.

Royal Prestige made me a trainer and then a a manager, I was running offices in Louisville, Nashville, and Atlanta. But the more money I made the less content I was. After seven years of this, I had had enough. I was tired of going door to door. I was tired of selling the same stories. More than that, I was tired of selling over-priced cookware to young women who could never afford it.

This is how it worked at Royal Prestige. If you couldn't pay cash, you could apply for credit. When you applied for credit, you also got a credit card. And if you were a young woman eighteen years of age, you got credit on the spot. No questions asked.

The girls were always excited about the credit card, until they learned it wasn't a Visa or MasterCard. It was a Royal Prestige card, good only for buying Royal Prestige products. On the other hand, the debt you accrued from buying the cook set you couldn't afford was just as real as any other debt, and it set many of those young women up to fail, as they could not afford the payments.

Being a salesman made me a lot of money. I was damn good at what I did, and I still have the plaques and trophies to prove it. But let's face it, I wasn't born to be a salesman. I was born to be in the wrestling business. The business had dealt me a bad hand thus far, but things were about to change.

I FINALLY GET MY BIG BREAK, NO THANKS TO JIMMY

We're coming up to the part you've all been waiting for, the moment I finally enter the wrestling business. But first, it's time for a flashback. If you haven't picked up on this already, this is how I tell stories. I start one story, I jump forwards or backwards to another, then I come back to finish the first story. I may jump around a lot, but I promise I won't start a story without finishing it! (And if I do, we'll blame it on Cosper for not catching it!)

If there was any doubt in anyone's mind that I was meant to be in the wrestling business, the doubts were crushed and maimed in 1976. That was when I, Kenny Bolin, booked my first wrestling match at the Louisville Gardens for Nick Gulas and Roy Welch, the Memphis promoters. It was a star-studded affair featuring Jerry "The King" Lawler, then the most hated man in town, and Coyote Calhoun.

"Wait a minute, Mr. Bolin. Coyote Calhoun? I don't remember a wrestler named Coyote Calhoun!" That's true. Coyote Calhoun was not a wrestler. At the time Calhoun was the evening disc jockey on 790 WAKY AM, the most popular top 40 radio station in town. He would later move to WAMZ, Louisville's number one country station, where he won multiple awards as a disc jockey and a station manager. Calhoun is a bona fide legend in radio, not just in Louisville, but across the country, and in 1976, yours truly got him to wrestle.

Coyote Calhoun was known for taking challenges from his fans. The WAKY-AM guys all served as guest announcers for wrestling on Tuesdays, so I figured why not challenge Calhoun to take on Lawler in a wrestling match? I called into the station one night and laid out the challenge. Soon Calhoun and Lawler were exchanging verbal barbs on the air, and next thing you knew, Coyote Calhoun was booked to face off with Jerry "The King" Lawler at the Louisville Gardens.

Jim Cornette

Calhoun agreed to face Lawler as long as he could use his "Bohemian Alligator Holt". Lawler of course agreed, and the match was set. One night on the air, tens of thousands of listeners were treated to the audio of Coyote's workout, applying the "Holt" to a man who screamed in agony.

When the match was finally announced for November 28, there was incredible interest to see what would happen when a six foot, 130 pound hippie like Coyote fought the King of Wrestling. Unfortunately, the show was canceled due to a huge snowstorm and rescheduled for December 7.

A sell-out crowd was on hand in early December to see Calhoun come to the ring to confront Lawler with a bag of lollipops because he was the "biggest sucker in the world." Calhoun then introduced Lawler and the world to his "Bohemian Alligator Holt," a giant, 250 pound wrestler in green mask and trunks with his name in green letters on his T-Shirt. Lawler went nuts. He had so much heat with the local crowd, the Gardens was now solidly behind Calhoun and the unknown Holt.

The Holt wrestled almost the entire match. Lawler took bump after bump and made Holt look like a million dollars. Seven minutes in, Coyote made the mistake of tagging in. Lawler picked him up in an airplane spin, dumped him to the mat, and pinned him in about 15 seconds.

Kenny

My mother never owned car in her life, and week after week, I got to the matches thanks to a lady from LaGrange named Lola. I won't give her last name here for reasons that will soon become apparent. Lola knew I loved wrestling, so she started giving me a ride every Tuesday night to the Gardens. It was convenient for Lola, too because she soon was banging Tommy Marlin.

Our weekly trips to Louisville Gardens weren't enough for either of us, and soon we were also making the trek to Evansville Wednesdays, Lexington Thursday, and even Memphis on Saturday. Back then there was no Internet, so the boys would do the same exact show at each stop during the week. The show the fans saw in Memphis Monday was repeated, right down to the finish, on Tuesday in Louisville, Wednesday in Evansville, and so on.

One night during the show, Lawler pulled Jimmy aside in a back stairwell. Jim could tell right away that Lawler was pissed.

"What the fuck do you think you're doing?" said Lawler. "Why the fuck have you been telling people the finishes to every match?"

Jimmy was stunned. "Jerry, I swear, I would never do that! You know me, I love this business, and I'd never, ever do that!"

61

"No one else is going to the matches in Louisville, Evansville, and Memphis!" said Lawler. "So who is it?"

"I swear, it's not me, Jerry!" said Jim.

Jerry loosened his grip on Jim. "Maybe you need to have a talk with your friend Kenny."

My phone rang at 3 AM that night. I've heard Jim pissed off many times before and since, but that night was the worst I ever heard him. He was convinced I was running my mouth, giving away the finishes, something I would never do any more than he would. Right then and there on the phone, he threatened to end our friendship for good.

Oh the years of pain and suffering that might have spared me!

Then it hit me. I had heard Lola talking to some of the other ladies at the matches in recent weeks, telling them the finishes. "Dundee's going to do this, and the other guy will do that, and this is how it will end." Much as I appreciated Lola for giving me a ride, she nearly cost me big time running her mouth.

While Lola caused Jimmy and I both a lot of grief that night, I have Lola to thank for my close, personal friendship with Jerry Lawler. After the matches in Louisville, Tommy hopped in the car with Lola, who drove him and some of the boys to their favorite liquor store. I wasn't allowed to ride along on these runs, so Lawler would give me a ride to McDonalds for Big Macs and Big Reds. Lawler was one of the few wrestlers who never drank, and he was glad to have a "drinking buddy" with similar taste in beverages.

One time we were in the gas station when Rocky Johnson, the Rock's dad, walked in. Jerry went ballistic. He was in the midst of a feud with Rocky, with Rocky playing the babyface and Jerry playing the heel. Babyfaces were not supposed to be seen with heels in public, ever. I thought Jerry was going to fire the man on the spot!

Jerry was just a teenager when he became friends with Jackie Fargo, the man who got him into the wrestling business. I often thought Jerry would do the same for me, but I was never bitter he never made any offers. Then to my surprise, the other Jerry of Memphis wrestling made an offer to another teenager instead of me.

One afternoon at lunch, Memphis promoter and owner Jerry Jarrett got the bright idea to turn Jim Cornette, photographer, into Jim Cornette, manager. He was sitting a few tables away listening to Cornette flap his gums, and he this close to shoving his fist down the boy's throat to make him shut up. The wily promoter suddenly realized that he had a Grade A, bona fide heel manager right under his nose. Not long after, Jimmy traded in his camera for a tennis racket and the rest is history.

No one was more excited than I to see Jimmy get his break. I was glad to see my pal move from the arena floor to the center of the ring. It was a dream come true for Jim. More importantly, it was a dream come true for yours truly. I knew for sure that once Jimmy established himself, he'd find a way to get his old pal Kenny into the business. Right? RIGHT??

Boy was I a chump!

Cornette never did a thing for his old friend, his one true friend in all the world. When I asked, Jim told me he didn't want to use his connections (like he had so many!) to bring me in. He told me I needed to "pay my dues" and "work my way up" and a bunch of other nonsense they tell to the wrestlers who are never, ever gonna make it.

It's not because I wasn't wanted, of course. As a matter of fact, my first invitation to join the wrestling business came from none other than Randy Savage. Yes, THE Randy Savage, the Macho Man, the Macho King, the world's biggest Slim Jim fan. Macho's career took off right here the Bluegrass State. In 1978 Randy's father Angelo Poffo started International Championship Wrestling in Lexington, Kentucky. Angelo built the promotion around his sons, Randy and "Leaping Lanny" Poffo, who would later work in the WWF as The Genius. He surrounded the boys with some talented workers including my future OVW co-worker Rip Rogers, Buddy Landel, Ox Baker, "The One Man Gang" Ron Garvin, and Bob Orton, Jr. Incidentally, Bob's son Randy was born in Lexington during his Dad's stint with ICW.

ICW had a world of talent but they just couldn't catch a break with the Kentucky fans. They didn't draw even a fraction of what Jerry Jarrett's crew did in Lexington, and Lexington was Jarrett's weakest town. ICW didn't do themselves any favors with the way they constantly brought up Memphis on television and at their house shows. Announcer Bob Roop would tell the fans to write Jerry Jarrett and demand to see Bill Dundee versus Leaping Lanny and Jerry Lawler versus Randy Savage.

Wrestling promotion 101 friends: If you go out to the ring and mention the name of the rival promotion in your town, you have just made yourself second fiddle to that promotion!

Back to my story, one day I received a letter from Randy Savage asking me to join ICW. I kid you not! The partially handwritten, partially typed letter remained one of my prized possessions until it was lost in a house fire. To be honest, I was a bit surprised by the offer. I had no experience in the wrestling business to that point, but Randy knew I was tight with Cornette, Lawler, and the Jarretts. Most likely he saw in me a chance to strike a blow at their wrestling family and steal one of their own!

I gave serious thought to joining up with the Poffos, but before giving an answer, I took the letter to Christine Jarrett. "Teeny," as we all knew her, was Jerry's mother, and when the Memphis crew went on the road, she was the boss. Her word carried a lot of weight with everyone, including yours truly, so I listened when she spoke.

"You can go," said Christina Jarrett, "But if you do, you will sever all ties with us. You will not be welcome back, and you will never work here."

Truth be told, there was only one man I wanted to work for at that time, and it was Jerry Jarrett. I consider the man to be one of the greatest minds in wrestling history and one of my mentors. I declined the offer, trusting that Miss Christine would honor my loyalty and open the doors wide for me.

I don't blame Miss Christine or her son for the fact that it was another eight years until my big break came. I lay that blame solely at the feet of Jim Cornette. He was their little prodigy, and I'm sure it was he who made sure the door stayed closed to me. Jim kept telling me it was for my own, good, but I knew whose good he was looking out for.

I had no doubt I would make it. I knew I'd be a killer manager, hell even better than skinny young Cornette! I also knew that there was no way in hell I was gonna "pay dues." I was gonna get my break and break out, just like Jim.

I was right.

Flash forward to the tail end of my days at Royal Prestige. I was living in Nashville at the time when I finally got my big break in the customer service lane at Service Merchandise.

For those who don't remember, Service Merchandise was a wonderland of jewelry, high end electronics, and other fine goods. Instead of picking up a box on the floor and taking it to the register, you'd take a tag beneath the item you wanted and take that to the register. After making your purchase, you proceeded to the pick up area, where they'd call for your item and send it down a big, long chute.

I was living in Nashville at the time, and I had recently purchased two brand new stereo receivers from this very store. I'd heard people saying that there was truly no difference between, say, a $150 receiver and a $700 receiver, so in the interest of consumer research, I picked up one of each to try out for myself. After testing both machines, I came to the conclusion that the $150 machine was just as good as the more expensive one, so I repacked the $700 box and took it back to the store. Only later did I discover that, due to both receivers being nearly the exact same size, I had inadvertently packed the $150 receiver in the $700 box.

But I'm getting ahead of myself. There I was in line at the customer service counter. I had my stereo in hand, carefully resealed as if it were brand new. I happened to glance back at the folks behind me, and right in the middle of that line was none other than Nick Gulas.

For those who don't know their Memphis wrestling, Nick Gulas and his partner Roy Welch were the promoters for the Memphis territory for years prior to Jerry Jarrett's arrival. After expanding the territory north to Louisville, Evansville, and Lexington, Jarrett eventually decided he no longer needed Gulas and Welch, and he definitely did not need Gulas's no-talent son George. Jarrett broke ties with them in 1978. Gulas tried to run against his former employee in Memphis and Louisville, but he eventually ceded the territory to Jarrett.

I allowed a few people to pass me so that I could make Mr. Gulas's acquaintance. I introduced myself to Nick, and he was very friendly. I was sure to drop some names of some famous friends of mine, like Jerry "The King" Lawler of course, and Nick was very impressed with me. Gulas began to talk to me about his own promotion in Nashville, and next thing I knew, I was offered a tryout to become an on air announcer.

Suck on that, Cornette!

Gulas had to have seen something in young Kenny Bolin that day. How do I know? Because my first assignment was an on-air interview with none other than George Gulas. If you're not familiar with George Gulas, let me fill you in. I've been fortunate to work with some amazing talents over the years, and I've stood side by side and toe to toe with the best. George Gulas stands alone, apart from all of these talents, at the very bottom of the heap.

George Gulas is the reason the southern part of the Memphis territory was dying in the late 1970's. George Gulas is the reason Jerry Jarrett broke away from Nick Gulas and Roy Welch in 1978. George Gulas was a disaster from the moment he laced up his wrestling boots. But that day, standing by my side, George Gulas looked like a million bucks.

The Starmaker was still an unknown, but he was already living up to his future nickname. I thought for sure that once Jimmy saw how successful I had become all on my own, he'd be more than willing to help me continue my success. Yes, after all Jim had done, I still naively believed that our childhood friendship still meant something to him.

As many of you die hards know, Jimmy had a little accident in a match involving his Midnight Express and the Road Warriors. It was a scaffold match, a very dangerous gimmick match first performed by Jerry Jarrett and Don Greene in my hometown back in 1971. A twenty-foot high scaffold was erected over the ring, and the two tag teams did battle on the scaffold. The first team to toss both of their opponents from the scaffold is the winner.

Somehow, someone convinced Jimmy to climb up on that scaffold his damn self. The plan was for Jim to dangle from the scaffold and be caught by the late Ray Traylor, who would later become the Big Boss Man in WWF. Unfortunately for Jim, Traylor didn't catch him in time and Jim blew both his knees out.

I saw a golden opportunity in that moment. Jim would be out of action four to six weeks easy, leaving the Midnight Express without a leader. I called Jim to offer my services as a fill in. Not only would I be able to keep things hot in Jimmy's absence, we would have a great story to tell when he came back. The two of us would go head to head for the Midnight Express. It was a tailor-made feud guaranteed to put butts in the seats.

As successful as I had become working for Gulas, I thought for sure Jim would jump at the chance to have a barn burning feud with his old pal, but Jim said no. He didn't even bother to check with the booker! He just flat out said no.

Jim and I could have done business together, years before OVW. We could have stayed friends. But Jim was so insecure, he chose to feud with Bobby Heenan and Paul Heyman. Heenan I could understand, but Heyman? Hell, that man screwed more people than I ever did, including Jim! I guess it's true what they saw that you reap what you sow.

Terry Garvin Simms

I met Kenny working for Nick Gulas of all people. Even at a young age he had a mind for business. He made some good decisions and some bad. But when it came to working the wrestling business, he was always gold.

I've never told anyone this, but I used to call Kenny for advice when I was getting ready for a big match. That's how much I believe in Kenny. When I first went to work in Texas, they made the legendary Freebird Buddy Roberts my manager. I asked and begged them to bring in Kenny to work as my manager. Nothing against Buddy, of course; Buddy was a legend. The office wouldn't go for it because Kenny wasn't well known as a manager, but I knew that if I had Kenny by my side, he would make me a national star. It's sad to me it took so long for Kenny to be recognized as a groomer of champions, but look at John Cena and all the other talents he trained! He made them into stars!

JIMMY DOES SOMETHING TERRIBLE

Later on in this book I will tell you how I, Kenny Bolin, became the real pioneer in Internet podcasting. Long before Steve Austin, Jim Ross, Chris Jericho, and even Colt Cabana had their shows, I was the top rated segment on Tommy Fiero's podcast with my weekly update, the Bolin Alley. My success was due in no small part to the story I must tell you now, a story that once and for all answers the greatest mystery in professional wrestling history: Who screwed Bret?

Unless you just started watching wrestling a week ago, you know the story of the Montreal Screwjob. Bret "Hitman" Hart, the WWF's top star and World Champion, had a multi-million dollar offer on the table from the WWF's arch-rival, WCW. Vince McMahon had already told Bret he was not going to match the offer, and it was all but settled that Bret would finish his contract with the WWF and head for WCW. The only question was, how would Bret drop the title before he left?

The war between WWF and WCW was nearing its peak of ugliness. Already Vince McMahon had witnessed former Women's Champion Alundra Blayze showing up on WCW television and throwing the WWF Women's Championship Belt in the trash can. Vince did not want to see the same thing happen with the biggest prize in his company.

Bret had vowed to do the honors and drop the belt on his way out, but Bret had told Vince he would not drop the belt in Canada. A native of Canada himself, Bret did not want to lose his title in his native country, so when Vince asked him to do the honors at Survivor Series in Montreal on November 9, 1997, Bret politely declined, offering to drop the belt the next night on Raw instead.

Bret put Vince in a difficult spot. Could he trust Hart to fulfill his word and show up to Raw the next night? Or would WCW mastermind Eric Bischoff score the greatest coup in wrestling history and get Bret to dispose of the WWF title on WCW Monday Nitro?

Vince didn't take the chance. At the end of the match, Vince made his way to the ring with a few of his stooges on tow. Shawn Michaels, Bret's opponent and backstage rival, put Bret into Bret's signature finisher, the Sharpshooter. It was planned all along that Shawn would use the Sharpshooter on Bret before Bret kicked out, reversed the hold, and got the win. What Bret didn't know was that he wouldn't be given the chance to kick out. As soon as Shawn locked on the Sharpshooter, Vince McMahon called for the bell. Bret never tapped out, but the match was called as a victory for Shawn. Referee Earl Hebner, who was in on the scheme from the beginning, headed out a side door and into a waiting car. Triple H escorted his buddy Michaels to another waiting car with the belt. Bret and the Montreal fans were left in shock and disbelief at what happened.

What transpired in the ring is without dispute. It was documented by WWF cameras and has been discussed at great lengths in shoot interview after shoot interview. What was never revealed - until I revealed it on the podcast - is who gave Vince the idea to screw Bret.

I think you can probably guess already.

Jimmy called me a few weeks prior to Survivor Series, telling me all about the WCW contract situation with Bret. Vince wasn't worried about the matter at the time, but Jimmy was determined to make him worry. Jim didn't trust Bret. He was certain Bret was going to betray Vince the same as Alundra Blayze. He wanted Vince to take action, to do something.

As Jimmy kept on talking, it became clear to me Jim wasn't nearly as concerned about Bret as he was himself. You see, by this point in his career, Jimmy's managing days were winding down. Jim didn't have the Midnight Express, the Heavenly Bodies, or Yokozuna under contract any more. Jim was still an important figure backstage, but he was now more or less one of Vince's stooges, just another former wrestling guy Vince kept around to toss out ideas. The one guy still loyal to Jim was Bret Hart's younger and more talented brother, Owen Hart, and therein lay the reason for Jim's "concerns" about Bret.

Jim was already looking far beyond Survivor Series to the biggest show on the WWF calendar, Wrestlemania. In previous conversations, Jim had shared with me what the pay offs were for the big event. "Do you know, the guys in the main event usually take over a million dollars home? A million bucks, Kenny! And a guy managing the main event? That's worth at least $350,000!"

Putting two and two together, I could the see scheme percolating in Jim's mind. Had Bret not signed with WCW, he likely would have held the belt until Wrestlemania, where he would finally drop it to Michaels. If Bret were to be out of the picture, the WWF would have a main event hole to fill. Who better to fill a spot vacated by Bret Hart than his brother

Owen Hart? And who better to make sure that happened than Owen's manager Jim Cornette?

I asked Jim what he was planning, curious to know how far he would go to get his $350,000 payday. Jim didn't have a plan, but he said he would get back to me. For the next two weeks, he would call every couple of days with an update. No, he didn't have a plan. No, he didn't know what Vince would do. But he remained steadfast in his previous declaration: Bret Hart could not leave Montreal with the WWF World Championship Title.

I thought Jimmy was just blowing smoke. I had no idea he would actually try and take action against a man of Bret's stature and talent. But the afternoon of the pay-per-view, I received one more call from Jim Cornette.

"Kenny," he said, "Watch for the sharpshooter."

"What?" I said.

"Watch for the sharpshooter," he said with a laugh. "Just watch for it." He hung up.

I was puzzled. The sharpshooter, as I already told you, was Bret's signature finishing move. When Bret locked into the sharpshooter, that was the match. No one ever got out of the sharpshooter. Ever. I never would have guessed that Jim meant that Shawn would use the sharpshooter to steal the title from Bret!

Guess what? Shawn did use the sharpshooter, and it was all Jimmy's idea. After years of working backstage for McMahon, Jim had learned that the last stooge to get a word in with Vince before show time was the guy most likely to get his idea used on the show. Jim let Jerry Briscoe, Pat Patterson, and all the other stooges get their moment with Vince before he stepped in and told McMahon what he had to do for the finish. "Have Shawn put Bret in the sharpshooter, then ring the bell. Tell Earl. Tell Shawn if you want. Maybe tell Triple H so he can get Shawn to high ground. They're the only ones who need to know."

It went down just as Jimmy planned. Jim Cornette screwed Bret Hart. As soon as Vince called for the bell, Shawn Michaels, Earl Hebner, and Jim Cornette all ran like hell. Vince stayed to take the heat and a hard right to the jaw from Bret.

Jim Cornette

What do I have to say in response to Kenny's allegations? Kenny Bolin is a fucking liar. That's all I have to say. That, and Vince Russo couldn't even spell screwjob if you spotted him the first seven letters.

Kenny Bolin

The ironic twist to the story is that son of a bitch never got his Wrestlemania main event. Shawn Michaels went on to Wrestlemania as champion, but it was "Stone Cold" Steve Austin who took the title in a match called by guest referee Mike Tyson. Jim Cornette, the man who screwed Bret Hart, got to jerk the curtain as manager of The New Midnight Express. His boys were the last team eliminated in a tag team battle royal won by LOD 2000 featuring Road Warriors Hawk and Animal and their manager Sunny.

Small wonder Jim wanted to get out of Stanford so bad in the late 1990s.

FROM BAD TO ROTTEN

Working for Nick Gulas was exciting, exhausting, and frustrating. I started off at the announcer's desk, but soon found myself working as a manager, ring announcer, and building manager. I was eager to learn, and Nick was more than glad to let me wear as many hats as I wanted. The more I did, the less work he and his good for nothing son had to do!

The Nick Gulas promotion that gave me my break was nothing like the glory days of the 1970s. Tojo Yamamoto and Gypsy Joe were two of the top stars in a very underwhelming locker room. Truth be told, Nick really only went into business just to say he was still on television. he couldn't compete with the declining Jerry Jarrett Memphis promotion, much less the WWF, and his pay offs reflected that.

Like many people, Gulas hired me in the hopes that I would become a lure for my childhood friend, Jim Cornette. Remember that, folks, because you will soon see that becomes a trend in my career. Nick hired me on at the agreed upon rate of $250 a week, and I would soon discover that getting money out of Nick Gulas was an even greater challenge than getting into the business.

After not receiving any payment for some time, I drove down to Nashville. I went to Nick's house and knocked on the door. After a long pause, his son George answered the door.

"What can I do for you, Kenny?" he said.

"I need to see your dad," I said.

"Dad's not here," said George.

"I'm here to collect my pay," I told him.

"Well, you're gonna have to talk to dad about that," said George.

"When's your dad gonna be home?" I asked.

"A couple hours," said George.

I said farewell and left the house. A few hours later, I went back. No surprise, George answered the door again.

"Sorry, Kenny, dad's not back yet," he said.

"You said he'd be back in a few hours," I said.

"I know," said George. He went on to make excuses for a bit, but as he spoke, I caught sight of the elder Gulas crossing through the living room behind him.

"George," I interrupted, "I know he's home. I just saw him."

"No, no, dad's not here," said George.

"Stop lying, George," I said. "He just walked through the living room."

George flinched. "Okay, give me a second. Let me see if he just got back."

George shut the door, leaving me on the porch. Several minutes later, the door opened, and Nick Gulas greeted me.

"Hello, Kenny," he said. "What can I do for you?"

"I'm here to get paid," I said.

"Oh, right," said Nick. "Listen, cash is a little tight right now. Can I give you thirty bucks?"

"You owe me $250," I said.

"Look," he said. "Take thirty now, and I'll get you the rest soon, I promise."

I took the thirty and left. A week or so later, I went back to Nashville to get the same run around. This time I walked away with seventy dollars. When the boys in the locker room heard this, they were actually impressed. "Congratulations," they said, "You're probably the only guy ever to get a hundred bucks out of Nick who wasn't already an established player in the business."

I stayed on with Nick for a few months, but being the frugal man I am, I eventually decided it wasn't worth my time. I told Nick I was done, and I left the business I had dreamed of entering for nine years.

The next several years were spent on the outside, save for some work I did for Jimmy. Jim opened his own promotion based in Knoxville, a beloved little upstart he called Smokey Mountain Wrestling. Smokey Mountain ran shows in Tennessee, Kentucky, West Virginia, Virginia, and North Carolina.

Jim basically recycled everything he ever learned from Jerry Jarrett. It worked because the Smokey Mountain territory for the most part never saw Memphis wrestling and didn't realize every idea was recycled. Jim recruited well, I must admit, and a few future stars came out of SMW, including Lance Storm, Chris Jericho, Sunny, Chris Candido, Bob Holly, and Kane.

Jim used me when he had to as a ring announcer and building manager, but he was careful not to give me too much control. Jim had no more experience as a promoter than I did, and the last thing he wanted was for his old buddy to snatch his baby out from under him.

One day, out of the blue, I got a call from my old pal Dennis Corralluzzo. Corralluzzo asked if I might be free for dinner one night, and I agreed to meet him at Kingfish on the river. What happened at that dinner would bring me back into the wrestling fold for good.

Corralluzzo was one of the big shots on the East Coast with the International Wrestling Association. IWA was broken into smaller sub-territories across the country, and they had decided to open an office dubbed IWA Mid-South in Louisville.

The man chosen to run the show was ECW veteran Ian Rotten, the kayfabe brother of fellow ECW star Axl Rotten. Ian was an East Coaster himself with a reputation for being in some of the bloodiest hardcore matches on record. Corralluzzo needed someone to look over Ian's shoulder, to be his eyes and ears in town. "I can't be here every week," he told me. "I need someone I can trust to assist Ian."

I told Dennis I would do it, only if Ian agreed to pay me $75 per week. Dennis got in touch with Ian, and when Ian agreed to the deal, Corralluzzo arranged another meeting between myself and Ian.

Believe it or not, in the mid to late 1990s, it was IWA Mid-South, not Ohio Valley Wrestling, that was the hottest ticket in town. Danny was working out of the Quadrangle in Jeffersonville, a dilapidated former army storage depot that has since been renovated. It was a dive, and he was lucky to draw any fans at all. Ian found himself a few "money marks," fans with money who weren't too bright, and managed to secure and renovate the old Kmart building on Dixie Highway. He had the better building, and he had a rabid, loyal fan base that followed him like a cult leader. His fans call themselves "Kool-Aid drinkers," if that tells you anything!

One of my best moves in a wrestling ring happened at IWA Mid-South. Somehow I found myself in the ring with Mad Man Pondo, a man so insane he once let another person body slam him onto a bed of sharpened number two pencils. I was supposed to give Pondo an arm drag toss, a move I could do very well left-handed. I'm a natural leftie, so the few moves I learned, I learned to do left-handed.

When Pondo came at me in the ring, he came at me for a *right-* handed arm drag. I had no idea how to execute the move right handed, so I quickly flung my left arm at Pondo and hooked him high in the air, tossing him over my body. It was the worst arm drag in the history of wrestling, but even Ian had to laugh about it.

Ian was thrilled to have me on board. Corralluzzo sold me to Ian as "Jim Cornette's best friend," and like Nick Gulas before him, Ian was hopeful that connecting with me would allow him to connect with Jim.

Ian wasn't the only one hoping for big things from my well-connected friend. Everyone in the locker room looked after me and kissed up to me. One night I took a hard bump in the ring from Bull Pain. It hurt me pretty bad, but truthfully... not that bad. I decided to sell the hell out of it anyway as I left the building that night.

Bull was really upset about it. He really thought he had hurt me. The next day, he called me up. "Hey, Kenny, how are you feeling?"

"Oh Bull," I croaked out in a faint, pained voice. "Thank you so much for calling. I think I'm done. I may never wrestle again. I can't even afford to go to a doctor and get checked out."

"Is there anything I can do for you?" asked Bull. "Anything at all?"

"Yeah," I said. "Bring me some damn ice cream."

"Sure thing, Kenny," he said. "What kind do you want?"

I told him the brand, the flavor, everything. Bull said, "Okay, okay, Kenny. Anything else?"

"Yeah," I said in my regular voice. "Quit being such a damn mark. I'm fine!!"

Truthfully, Jimmy showed a little interest when he heard I was working with IWA Mid-South. Jim was getting tired of the politics at WWF headquarters in Connecticut. He hated the East Coast, and he wanted to return to his mansion in Prospect.

"Listen, Jimmy," I told him, "Ian's got some talented kids here. He's got a nice building and a loyal following. Now that Memphis is no more, this might be a place for the WWF to send guys who need a little seasoning."

At that time the idea of creating a developmental territory had not yet been broached. Vince McMahon started his expansion in the 1980s by cherry picking the old territories. Once those dried up, he started sending guys to Jerry Jarrett in Memphis, future stars like Kane and the Rock. With Memphis no longer an option, a place like IWA could have been an ideal solution.

There was just one hang up: Ian Rotten. Ian was a hardcore guy, and he brought the hardcore style to Louisville. Every week, he fed his fans a steady diet of hardcore fare featuring barbed wire, fluorescent light tubes, and other assorted weaponry. That bloodlust helped to build his fan base, but it ultimately led to his banishment from the state of Kentucky.

Jim Cornette

Ian was called to testify in Frankfort before a bunch of politicians. He cut a promo on the Kentucky State House, trying to convince them that wrestling was art and if he wanted to stab someone in the head with barbed wire, that was his business. Dick the Bruiser did the same thing back in the 1960s in Indianapolis, but the Kentucky law makers didn't buy it like the Indiana law makers did. Thanks to Rotten, Kentucky went from being one of the most lenient states in regards to professional wrestling to one of the toughest. Nowadays I can't even set foot in the ring without a license and submitting to random drug testing! Rotten also got himself banned from working in the state of Kentucky and had to move across the river to Indiana.

Kenny

Jim started feeding me ideas to take back to Ian, just to see if he'd play ball. It was a lost cause, right from the start. Ian Rotten listens to no man other than himself. He was not about to take story direction from anyone, be it myself, Jim Cornette, or Dennis Corralluzzo. He steadfastly refused to tone down the blood and gore, and he continued to bring in some of the sickest minds in the business to keep pushing the envelope.

He would not cut back the number of matches on his shows either, packing as many as 14 matches into one night. It wasn't uncommon for us to start at 7:30 and wrap up a show around 1 or 2 am.

All talent had to wait until the very end of the show to get paid. Once the building was cleared, we got in a line, and one at a time, we went into Ian's private office to receive our payment, via the "secret handshake" pass.

Many wrestlers have made claims over the years about Ian short paying them or not paying them at all. Rumor was if you were at the end of that line at 2 AM, there might not be any cash left by the time you received your handshake. I can honestly say that as long as I was working for him, Ian paid me what he promised. We said $75 a week, and he paid me $75 a week as long as I was there. I'm pretty certain that was three times the amount anyone else on the card was getting paid. I'm also certain that for as long as I worked for IWA Mid-South, I was at the front of the line when it came time to get paid!

FROM ONE "ROTTEN" PROMOTER TO ANOTHER

The peak of my popularity in IWA Mid-South coincided with the rise of the New World Order (NWO) in World Championship Wrestling (WCW). I and my boys started making our entrances to the NWO theme. One night I came out, and there were these four boys from UK wearing KWO T-shirts. What a thrill! I had never had a Kenny Bolin shirt, and here these boys had made their own. My only regret was I didn't have a piece of the action.

On closer inspection, the T-shirts were actually UK shirts purchased from the UK bookstore. The shirts said, "Kentucky World Order," but the boys had taken black tape and covered up "tucky." Within a few months there were about thirty of them, my own cheering section.

My success at IWA Mid-South opened another important door for me. Danny Davis of OVW came calling and offered me a spot as a manager and an announcer. Danny ran on different nights than Ian, so I gladly accepted.

Danny had no problem with me still working for Ian, but Ian wasn't thrilled with my decision to work for a rival promotion. One night, Joe Bailey warned me that Ian planned to hit the ring during a match I was managing and hit me with a Kendo stick. Soon as the three count was done in that match, I scooted to the back. Ian was shocked to see me back so quick.

"What the hell are you doing?" he said. "The match isn't over!"

"Yes, it is," I said. "There's nothing left for me to do out there." It wouldn't be the last time I would escape Ian's retribution.

Things were going much better for me at OVW in Jeffersonville, and I began to envision a day when I would leave the hardcore scene behind. Danny still had a shitty building, far worse than Ian's, but at least Danny wasn't nagging me to cut myself and bleed every week - something I never, ever did!

One day I got a call from OVW with an offer I could not refuse. If I left IWA Mid-South and worked exclusively for them, I would be their sole advertising sales agent. I'd get a cut of all advertising sales, work as an announcer and as a manager. After letting Danny Davis know I was aboard, I did the honorable thing and gave Ian Rotten my notice.

It almost cost me, big time.

Ian asked me to finish out an angle we had been working for some time. I agreed to do it, and we set the date for my final show. Ian was disappointed, but he never gave me any indication he was pissed at me. I was a sitting duck.

On my final night in IWA Mid-South, I went down to the ring with my boys, worked the match, and returned to the back without incident. Not a word was said about my departure. As was my custom at the time, I chose to stick around until the show was through. I had to get my payout, right?

Turns out Ian had more than a paycheck waiting for me. I was determined to give me a "receipt," wrestler speak for a beating meant to deliver a message.

Rick Brady, Promoter Premiere Destination Wrestling

Kenny was over huge with the fans at IWA Mid-South. The KWO was a big reason. Kenny had also stepped in and acted as the booker for a time while Ian was out of town. He was a little too good at it for Ian's taste. Ian wanted to punishing the King, but Kenny was one step ahead, as usual, and left before a receipt could be paid.

Kenny was always very good to me, treated me like a little brother. I actually was the recipient of his final tennis racket shot in IWA Mid-South.

Kenny

I didn't know the homicidal, genocidal Sabu very well. The nephew of the legendary Sheik was already a legend in his own right, especially among the hardcore faithful. He was a quiet man who didn't speak much, but that night, he found me backstage and pulled me aside.

"Ian's going to drag you out to the ring at the end of the night," he said. "He's going to make you bleed."

Ian had always wanted to make me bleed. Blood sport was his stock and trade. It's what made him a "legend." It was what put butts in the seats in the old Kmart building. He was always after me to blade and bleed like the rest of his Kool-Aid drinking crew. I myself never saw the point in the blood and gore, and I always politely declined. I wasn't about to bleed against my will.

I stuck my hand out and took Sabu by the hand. "Sabu," I said, "You're a good man. See ya." I grabbed my briefcase and got out of there, fast as I could.

Mad Man Pondo

It wasn't Sabu who warned Kenny. It was me. Ian asked Ox Harley and I to do the honors, dragging Kenny to the ring and beating the shit out of him. Kenny had never done anything wrong by me, so I warned him to get out.

Kenny

I was finally free of IWA Mid-South. I had my plum new job working with Danny Davis, and I could see myself becoming not just an employee, but a partner within a few short years.

Danny put me to work selling sponsorships for OVW. Thanks to my natural instincts for business, I had sponsors all over that building in no time at all, and companies were lining up to sponsor our television program.

Sylvester Terkay, former Bolin Services client

When I got to OVW, they were running out of a dump. It was an old army warehouse in Jeffersonville in a run down part of town. Somehow, Kenny was able to convince people to sponsor wrestling shows in that dirty old warehouse and convince them to sponsor our television program. He was always trading tickets, memorabilia, and WWE talent appearances for whatever we needed.

I don't know how big of a cut Kenny got from the ad sales, but I imagine Kenny had to be doing very well. Kenny had a big flat screen TV, way back before everyone else did. Matter of fact, he had seven or eight TVs in his living room and probably thirteen in his whole house. He easily had fifteen thousand dollars worth of televisions in his house, and yet he drove a thousand dollar car.

Kenny

OVW was a hit, and I was a big part of their success. But wouldn't you know it, as soon as I made OVW matter, Jimmy Cornette smelled an opportunity to come in and take it all away.

One day, out of the blue, Danny Davis announced that he had struck a deal with the WWF to become their official training center, and Jim Cornette would become Danny's partner in crime.

Talk about betrayal! Talk about a stab in the back! I thought Vince McMahon was good at stealing ideas and claiming they were his, but Jimmy? Jimmy had taken my concept, my vision for Louisville wrestling, and made it his own. Only instead of signing IWA Mid-South, he signed Danny Davis and OVW.

Jim Cornette

I was sick of the WWF and all the bullshit politics. I wasn't ready to quit the business, but I wanted out of the corporate office. I wanted to go home.

Over the Christmas holiday I ran into Danny Davis, who invited me to take a look at his training school in Jeffersonville. When I saw all Danny had going, the school, the travel, and the TV show, I saw an opportunity.

The WWF had Tom Pritchard working with some kids in a cold warehouse up near Titan Towers. It was a sad excuse for a training center and a far cry from the old territories that pretty much trained every major star the WWF had. OVW presented a unique opportunity to train new stars in an old school way. Jim Ross agreed, and I was on my way home.

Kenny

I was all over Ohio Valley Wrestling. I sold ads, I managed several wrestlers, and I worked the announcing table with Dean Hill, the legendary voice of Louisville wrestling. I did everything except own the place, and I didn't figure that was too far out of reach!

At the time OVW had a mix of young talent and old veterans, holdovers from the Memphis days like Rip Rogers, Flash Flanigan, and Trailer Park Trash. When the deal with WWE was struck, I saw changes coming. I knew the old guys would give way to new. I saw a real opportunity to not only advance some of my proteges to the next level, but to rise above OVW myself.

There was one thing I didn't count on: Jim Cornette.

I knew Jimmy was coming. I knew this whole developmental thing was his baby, and I knew we were going to be working together. For weeks I had tried to warn the fans that the Jim Cornette coming home was not the sweet teenager with the camera from twenty some odd years earlier. And what did the fans do? They ignored me and welcomed him with open arms!

At his first TV taping, he got into the ring and announced that changes were coming. Soon as he was done blowing hot air, I left my spot at the table to manage my boys in the first match of the night. Before the match could begin, Jimmy picked up the microphone.

"Kenny, I've got some good news," said Jim. "You don't have to worry about announcing any more. This is now my chair."

I was livid! Who the hell did he think he was, coming into my town, the town HE abandoned for the WWF, taking my seat? But the sneaky bastard wasn't done.

"And another thing. Those men you manage are property of OVW. They belong to us. You're fired!"

I blew a gasket! Not only did the son of a bitch steal my announcing gig, now he was taking away my wrestlers. I always knew he was jealous of me. He knew damn well I was the better man and the better manager, but I never dreamed he'd go so far as to take that away from me.

Next thing I knew, security had me by the arms and was leading me out of the building. The blowhard picked up the mic again for a parking shot.

"If you want to come back," said Cornette, "Go out and sign your own clients. Maybe then, we'll let you back in the building."

Maybe he didn't think I had it in me, but Cornette's words inspired me. Yes, I would be back. I would bring my own clients. I would get back in the building, and I would take over!

My come back began before I even left the parking lot. After suffering one more indignity when my OVW-appointed chauffeur walked away from me and my Cadillac to become Cornette's new driver, a man approached me. He was an imposing figure in a black suit, wearing a black fedora and black shades. He twirled a toothpick between his teeth as he looked down on me with a scowl.

"I understand you may be hiring," he said.

"I don't know who told you that," I said. "I've just been canned myself."

"And you're giving up?" he asked.

"No, sir," I said. "I may be down, but there's no way in hell I am out."

The man held out a hand. "My name's Black. Mr. Black."

I shook his hand. "You got a first name, partner?"

He shook his head. "Mr. Black will do."

I said, "Mr. Black, what is it you do?"

With a fiendish grin he told me, "I solve problems."

I could tell this was a man who knew how to handle himself in a fight, a man who would not take crap from skinny nerds like Jim Cornette, a man whose loyalty could easily be leased on a month to month basis.

"Mr. Black," I said, "This looks like the beginning of a beautiful friendship."

BOLIN SERVICES 1.0 IS BORN

A few hours later, Mr. Black and I were seated at a private table in one of Louisville's finer adult entertainment establishments. I was on the phone with Timmy John - you remember, my no good, good for nothing brother? - telling him all about Jim's betrayal and my plan to get revenge.

"What are you going to do?" said Timmy John.

"I'm going into business for myself," I said. "Mr. Black has a few contacts, and I plan to strike out and sign the toughest, meanest sons of bitches in the country. I'm going back to OVW as manager of the most dangerous faction the wrestling world has ever known."

"You got a name?" said Timmy John.

"Yes I do," I said. "Bolin Management."

The voice on the other end paused. "No good, Kenny. You go in with the initials 'B.M.' on your briefcase, and Cornette will be making bowel movement jokes at you."

Then Timmy John said the only wise, intelligent, and clever thing he has ever said in his life. "How about you call it, Bolin Services?"

I knew it was gold. "Timmy John, I believe you are on to something."

Bolin Services had a name. Now I needed some talent. Fortunately, my friend Mr. Black had a lead on my very first signing. Bright and early the next day, Mr. Black picked me up and drove me to the Kentucky State Penitentiary in Eddyville, Kentucky.

Warden Cletus T. Smithers

It ain't often that you see a big name celebrity come into the State Pen who isn't in handcuffs, but one day as I was making my rounds, I got a call that a former prison guard had arrived with the one and only Kenny Bolin. I cut my tour short and made my way back to the front office. I had always been a pro wrestling fan, and it was an honor just to stand in the presence of Mr. Bolin.

Black and Bolin had come hoping to make arrangements to sign one of our maximum security inmates. Mr. Buchanan, aka "Bull," had come to us recently after starting a riot at a lower security facility. Mr. Buchanan was personally responsible for assaulting the prison's head guard, who suffered a strained taint and a severely bruised medulla oblongata.

As much as I wanted to help Mr. Bolin, my hands were tied. Under the terms of Mr. Buchanan's sentence, he was ineligible for parole until 2015 or the cancellation of *24*, whichever came first. However, knowing Mr. Bolin was an upstanding citizen and a shaper of young men, we negotiated a deal with him and his attorney, Tim Denison.

Mr. Buchanan would be released on work assignment at Mr. Bolin's discretion any time Mr. Bolin needed him. That included all OVW events and television tapings, plus practice as required by Mr. Bolin and his assignees. We at the Kentucky State Penitentiary would provide transportation via armored van for Mr. Buchanan, who would be taken directly to work and promptly returned to prison once his work was concluded.

Eventually, Mr. Bolin was able to show that Mr. Buchanan had reformed himself, and parole was granted early. It's one of my proudest achievements that I was able to partner with Mr. Bolin in such a successful rehabilitation.

Kenny

Bull Buchanan had already been to the big dance, working most recently as a member of the Right to Censor faction in the WWF. Some legal trouble after his release landed him in Eddyville, but by the time we got to him, Bull was ready to turn his life around. In fact he had already reached out to Jim after hearing about the WWF developmental deal at OVW.

"Have you spoken to Jim?" I asked.

Buchanan shook his head. "I can't even get him to return my calls."

"Bull," I said, "You don't need Jim Cornette. You need me. I'm putting together a stable the likes of which the wrestling world has never seen. I want you to be in it."

Bull looked up. "Do you think you can get me back there? To the WWF?"

"You have my word on it," I said. We shook hands, and Bull Buchanan was a member of Bolin Services.

Having signed my first client, Mr. Black and I compiled a list of other names the WWF had recently cut. One name stood out immediately, and before the day was over, Mr. Black and I were on our way to Silsbee, Texas.

Silsbee is home to Mark Henry, the former Olympic weightlifter and world's strongest man. After a brief run with the WWF when he was known as "Sexual Chocolate," Mark was also cut loose. As we drove into the tiny Texas town of Silsbee, I hoped that Henry would be as eager as Buchanan to get back to the big time.

We found Mark working at a local cookware plant. Mark's job was to watch the assembly line for defective skillets and mash them up for recycling. When I say mash, of course, I mean with his bare hands. Years later Henry would perform this feat on WWF television, and millions of wrestling fans would roll their eyes in disbelief. "It's just a gimmicked skillet," they all said. Bullshit. Mark Henry is the world's strongest man. The skillet he crushed on Raw was as real and as solid as the four or five he mashed in front of Mr. Black and m while I spelled out my vision for Bolin Services.

"So you can get me back to the WWF?" he said.

"You, and anyone else who signs with me," I said.

Henry nodded, crinkling another skillet like it was a piece of paper. "All right, Mr. Bolin, I'm in."

I shook hands with Mark and left him to tie up loose ends with his employer and headed back to Houston. Our late evening flight was canceled, so Mr. Black and I checked into a hotel.

When Mr. Black and I went down for breakfast the next morning, the wrestling gods put another sign in my path - literally. As the elevator doors in the lobby opened, I saw one of the hotel staff set out a sign directing visitors to a workshop on sales and entrepreneurship entitled, "Chokeslam Your Next Million," led by none other than Sean O'Haire.

O'Haire was another former WWF talent, having entered the company after his previous employer WCW folded. O'Haire and Chuck Palumbo were the last team to win the WCW Tag Team Championship, a title they would quickly lose in the WWF. The two men were buried, lost in the shuffle of talent that became part of the WCW Invasion. When all was said and done, Palumbo got to stay and O'Haire got the shaft.

O'Haire was the star attraction in the Crockett Ballroom that day, speaking to entrepreneurs, account executives, and other suits on his controversial sales strategies for the 21st century. He looked razor sharp in his suit with the black on black shirt and tie, and he was as intense as ever in his delivery. The man even chokeslammed one of his paying guests during the presentation, which led to a premature end to the conference and a brief encounter with Houston police.

I got my good friend Tim Denison on the phone from Louisville to give O'Haire some impromptu counsel and assist him with the police. O'Haire was grateful and agreed to give Mr. Black and I a few minutes of his time before flying to Phoenix for his next presentation.

"How's business?" I asked him over a Blooming Onion at Outback Steakhouse.

"I'm loving it," said O'Haire. "I really feel like this is what I was made to do."

"Is that so?" I said. "You really want to spend the rest of your life speaking to sales people?"

He paused before answering. "Sure. I think so."

"You know you can't keep on body slamming your paid customers," I said.

O'Haire nodded. "Yeah. I guess old habits die hard."

"They don't have to die at all, Sean," I said. I went into my pitch, inviting O'Haire to sign on the dotted line. He continued to play coy with us, still trying to delude himself into the life of a motivational speaker. Long story short, he never did get on the plane for Phoenix. The next day, O'Haire flew first class with Mr. Black and myself back to Louisville, Kentucky.

When I arrived home, I discovered my answering machine was full of messages regarding a development a OVW. Rico Costantino, the first WWE signee to arrive in town, had gone down with an injury, and his future with the company was up in the air.

Those who only knew him by his WWE gimmick do not know my friend Rico. He was the first winner on the hit TV show American Gladiators. He was a high profile signee for the WWE, one they hoped to mold into the star of the future. But Rico received strike one the minute he flew into town. For some reason the WWE believed Rico was only 25. It wasn't until he arrived at Davis Arena that they learned he was 38 years young.

Going down with a torn quad (the same injury that famously struck Triple H live on Monday Night Raw) was strike two. By all accounts, Rico wouldn't even get the chance at a third swing.

Mr. Black and I high-tailed it to the hospital, flowers in one hand and a contract to the other. Rico was in low spirits when we found him, and while he was grateful for the visitors, Rico was leery of hearing what I had to say - not doubt to the influence of Jim Cornette.

"I appreciate you coming to see me, King B," said Rico. "But I think my best chances are staying with the Mr. Cornette right now."

I shook my head. "I appreciate your loyalty, son, but if I know Jimmy, he's already moved on. Give me six weeks after your injury heals, and I will make you a star. I guarantee it."

Rico signed, and true to my word, I made him bigger than he ever dreamed possible.

Bolin Services was a reality. Counting Mr. Black, I had assembled five men with more muscle, fire, and rage than the entire OVW locker room. I didn't think it was possible to go back to Louisville with a more dangerous collection of men.

Then again, I had no idea the biggest star in wrestling history was about to walk into my life.

I DISCOVER THE BIGGEST WRESTLING STAR EVER

Bolin Services took OVW by storm when I made my triumphant return. Right away, Mr. Black and Bull Buchanan captured the fabled Southern Tag Team Titles, a title BS was to carry in different combinations over the next decade. Cornette was clearly concerned when he saw the menagerie I had assembled. In fact I'm pretty certain he pissed himself a little that first night. It wouldn't be the last time Jimmy messed his pants at a TV taping. The night the Boogey Man debuted and Jimmy slapped the shit out of Santino Marella, he actually crapped his pants in the midst of his fury. Hand to God!

It wasn't all sunshine and roses, of course. Internally, Bolin Services had its issues, and Mark Henry nearly found himself back in Texas right away. Henry and I agreed to do a personal appearance at the Kentucky State Fair. The Fair takes place in late August, and if you've ever been to Louisville in late August, you know it's miserable hot that time of year. Henry, who had the eyes of the WWE on him once again thanks to me, scoffed at the idea of staying a full day in the blazing heat. When I told Henry he was staying whether he liked it or not, he told me to call Jim Ross, the legendary WWE announcer and (at the time) head of talent relations.

I got on the phone with Jim Ross right away. Ross is a good man who values discipline and loyalty in the talent he recruits, and when I explained the situation to Ross, he told me that he would rely on my wisdom in the matter. I hung up the phone and told Henry to pack his bags and head back to Silsbee.

A few days later Henry called me. He apologized for his ego, and he asked if he could return. I told him he would be returning to an even tighter ship. Whatever I said goes, or it would be his last shot at the big time. You can probably guess what the once and future Superstar decided to do. "I'll be there tomorrow," he told me. He was a model citizen from that day on as far as I was concerned.

Henry did a lot of damage around the Bluegrass, frequently battling head to head with Jim Cornette's feeble answer to the Bolin invasion, WWF Superstar The Big Show. Mr. Black and Bull Buchanan continued to dominate with the tag belts, and Rico and O'Haire were racking up bodies on their own. Still, something was missing. I didn't have that one guy, that mega-star who could put us over the top.

It happened one sunny afternoon at the old Davis Arena in Jeffersonville, Indiana. I was putting the boys through their drills when the back door opened and a man who looked like he had just stepped off a G.I. Joe package walked in the door. He was young, handsome, and in tip top shape. Matter of fact from the moment I laid eyes on him, I knew he was the prototype for the wrestling superstar of the future.

"Can I help you, son?" I said.

"Yes, sir," he said with a snap. "I'm looking for Jim Cornette. I understand he's the head of developmental for the WWE, and I want to be a WWE wrestler."

O'Haire leaned down and muttered in my ear. "This guy looks like GI Joe. He's not a wrestler."

Rico overheard Shaun. "Are you kidding me?" he said. "This guy's made for the WWE. Look at him. He's the... well, he's the Prototype!"

"That he is, Rico," I said. "Son, you don't want to see Jim Cornette. You want to see me."

"I do?" he said.

"My name is Kenny Bolin," I said with outstretched hand. "I'm the founder of Bolin Services. Perhaps you've seen us already on OVW television."

The young man glanced around at the man beasts now gathering around. "I see," he said.

"Son, look around you. This man won American Gladiators. This man was in the Olympics. This man already held gold in WCW. Do you know why they are here with me? Because I am the one who will send them straight to the top. Not in OVW, but in the world."

The young man grinned. "Mr. Bolin, you said?"

"That's right," I said. "And your name?"

I felt his vise-like hand lock on to mine. "My name is John Cena, and I want to be the world champion."

"John Cena," I said, "Welcome to Bolin Services."

A lot of folks have asked me over the years, what was John Cena really like? In all honesty Cena was the one man in my stable I knew the least. Most of the other boys spent hours at my house, enjoying my hospitality and learning from my many years of wrestling knowledge. We always invited Cena, of course, but Cena preferred to go home alone. Cena took advantage of the weekly stipend he collected once he was under contract with the WWE and ordered high speed internet. Cena was a big fan of, shall we say, streaming adult entertainment, and for some reason he preferred the virtual company he had online to the real company he could have had with us.

One night as the boy bounded for his car, I called out to him, "John, you're a good looking guy. You have WWE money in your pocket. You sure you don't want to go out and get the real thing with us?"

Extracurriculars aside, Cena was all business in the ring. He was far and away the best man to ever pick up a mic in Davis Arena. He could deliver promos backwards as well as he did forwards. Give him a topic or a scenario and he would shoot from the hip, delivering a pitch perfect promo every time with nary a stutter. Didn't matter if it was a fatal four way with Snap, Crackle, and Pop or a tag match with Rocky the Flying Squirrel, Cena nailed them all.

Cena was the trump card I needed in my battles with Jimmy Cornette. We billed him as the Prototype, a nod to his perfect physique and his flawless execution in the ring. Fans, you may know him as the arbiter of the "Five Moves of Death," but believe me, Cena has an arsenal far deeper than that! Cena could do anything, and did when he was at OVW. Now that he's the top dog in the WWE, it's his privilege to take fewer risks. That's the perk of being The Guy: you get paid more to do less.

He and Rico carried the tag titles for two months, and Cena held the OVW Championship for three months. True, in the end, Cena turned on me like an ungrateful child, forcing me to get in the ring with him and teach him a lesson. That's right, friends, Kenny Bolin got in the ring with John Cena - and

WON. It was a loser leaves town match, and I sent Cena packing.

Cena went on to the WWE and became the mega star I always knew he would be. He's still the ungrateful, unrepentant prodigal, the one member of Bolin Services I don't hear from on a regular basis, but that doesn't change history. It was Kenny Bolin who got him in the door, Kenny Bolin who made him a champ, Kenny Bolin who got him the attention of the WWE, and Kenny Bolin who made John Cena a star.

Liberty Elem. School   1971-72   Miss Black   Fifth Grade

That's me, fourth from the left in the front row. Smiling because I'd already talked half the class out of their lunch money that day, including Miss Black.

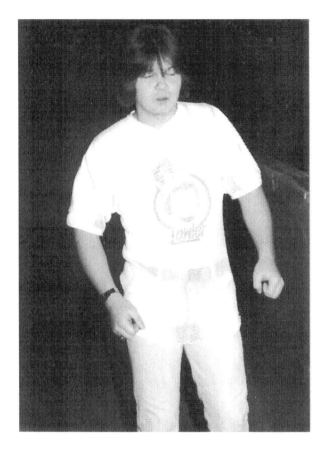

Wearing my first Jerry Lawler shirt.

Another Lawler shirt. Jim took this after we got back
from seeing some of Jerry's art at Wave 3. Cornette
took most of these, by the way.

Sitting front row at Louisville Gardens with Lisa Mudd, 1976. That might be James Garner behind us, but I doubt it.

Ready to score a deal on electronics.

Coming off the top of a chair against my old pal Mike Heilman. Corny took the pic. Nice action shot!

Me in 1978. I was a handsome devil.

My first prom date, Cindy Wedemeyer.

Taking Barbie Head to the prom. That damn Jim Cornette made me mow his lawn in exchange for taking photos.

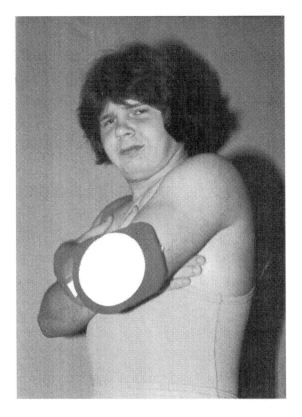

Didn't know I could wrestle, huh? That's right, kiss my ass!

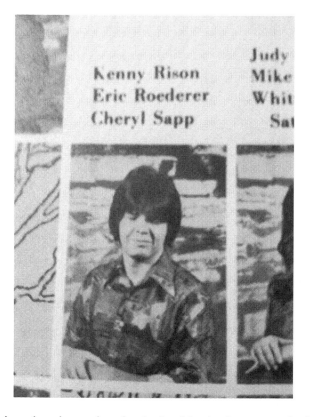

High school yearbook photo. Yeah, I was probably napping.

Two Kings. Told you we were pals.

With my first fiancee, Judy Koval.

Pre-Bolin Services days with the late, great Ron Wright. Black and white doesn't capture the glory of those orange and teal Miami Dolphin pants.

Destiny couldn't keep her hands off the King.

At the Eddie Gilbert Memorial in Philadelphia, 1997.

A dollar with a dollar with a dime. King, the late William "Paul Bearer" Moody, and some guy named Jim.

At my dad's summer home in North Carolina with
Chris and his mom, my ex Gabrielle.

The Prince in his first wrestling match vs. The King.

Backstage with Chris Theineman, James E., the Prince, and George Moore. Chris wrestled me that night, March 16, 1993 in Barbourville, KY. It was my son's birthday wish.

The ladies loved the Prince too. With the Dirty White Girl Kimberly.

The Prince and some friends posing with one of the
Undertaker's caskets.

Preparing for world domination!

Greatest tag team in OVW history: Rico and the
Prototype.

Yeah, that's me. And John Cena. No big.

My good buddy Nova vs. my most famous client.

With the Sean O'Haire.

The King, Lance Cade, Rene Dupree, and Sean
O'Haire. I really miss Lance and Sean.

With Mike Mondo and Carlito.

Featured in a wrestling comic strip from Germany.

Great piece of art by Joe Slack. This one's still hanging up at the OVW Danny Davis Arena in Louisville.

Just a few of the lives I've touched. You might
recognize a face or two.

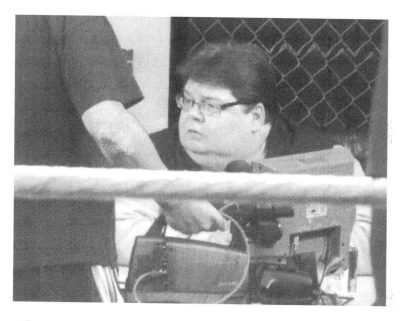

On color commentary. Who needs to rehearse? Not me!

Yes, I could smell what Jamin was cookin'.

With the legendary Dean Hill at the Danny Davis
Arena for OVW.

With Emmy award winner Gilbert Corsey.

DVD cover for a little picture starring me.

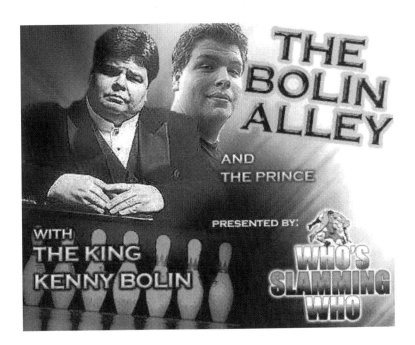

The King and Prince of Podcasts.

Shameless plug.

If you see this plate, you know your search for Beets
by Bolin is finally over.

At the ballpark with my daughter-in-law Mayara and the Prince. She couldn't be happier to be related to me.

Jim Cornette's abandoned bastard son, Little Jimmy LeBeau.

Choco the dog standing guard on the veranda out
back of Bolin Manor.

The incomparable Ma Bolin. Yes, folks, I gave her 5% off her shirt.

Biscuits and Gravy Raisor, my brother, the man of a thousand nicknames, and expert cockfight handicapper.

Still working. Still pleasing the fans. Still screwing
people like you.

Bolin Services was doing well at OVW. My clients were the best of the best, and my power was growing considerably. My bank roll was growing considerably as well, allowing me to indulge in some of the fineries of life. I bought myself a gold chain with a golden dollar sign and custom-tailored suits. If you want success, you have to dress for success, and friend, I knew how to dress.

John Bradshaw Layfield, WWE commentator and former World Heavyweight Champion.

I was backstage one night and Kenny came in wearing a new suit. It was like he lost a bet, or perhaps he dressed in the dark. He was either trying to be the #2 ball on a billiards table or try out for National Geographic as the Blue Whale. I assumed the #2 ball was not what he was going for, so he had to be a Blue Whale. The name stuck, or at least with me. From that day forward I only referred to Kenny as the Blue Whale. It seems to fit.

Bishop Jason Sanderson, "The Most Interesting Wolfman in New Hampshire"

During my first visit to meet Kenny Bolin, I have to say that I had the royal treatment; I was taken out to many nice restaurants and met a lot of really wonderful people. At each place, we never once were presented with a bill and at every restaurant we were greeted by the managers, personally.

Many people came over and talked about the shows, the opportunity for sponsorships, being ticket outlets and so forth. All vital services for any promotion, especially one that depended upon local support. In exchange for offers to set up meetings with the Office, or for a few complimentary tickets, our meals were free. By the time he brought me back to my hotel, my head was spinning from the number of places we had been and the number of people we had met.

The following day, I had a meeting with Danny Davis, Jim Cornette and Tom Prichard. I told them: "I don't know if Kenny has ever stepped foot in a ring or not, but by God he's the best 'worker' you guys have got in your entire promotion!"

Kenny

Despite all my success, I knew that I would never reach the heights I once enjoyed as long as Jim Cornette stood in my way. I needed someone bigger and badder than Cornette to help me reclaim what was rightfully mine - and maybe even more.

Mark Cuban was not the celebrity at the time that he is now. The self-made billionaire had only recently purchased the Dallas Mavericks, and he was years away from becoming a household name. Nevertheless, Mark Cuban had what I needed to take down Cornette: more money than Vince McMahon. Cuban was the one guy who could have bought out Vince with his pocket change.

I took a chance and called him. Hard as it is to believe, Cuban answered the call. I told him who I was and asked him if he'd be interested in being my partner in a takeover, first of OVW, then the WWE itself. I told him I had the Prototype, the greatest wrestler ever trained. Cuban was impressed, so we made plans to set up a meeting.

Cena didn't believe it was possible when I broke the news to him. He thought the Prince and I were ribbing him when we told him we had a date to meet with billionaire Mark Cuban. But on the scheduled day, a limousine arrived at my home and carried Cena, Chris, a cameraman, and myself to Indianapolis for a date with destiny.

The Mavericks were in town to play the Pacers that night, and Cuban had invited us up as his guests. Cuban really rolled out the red carpet for us. We ate with the players and even got to shoot around with Dirk Novitski and the rest of the Mavs. Everything was going well.

And then, it all fell apart.

At the appointed time, Cena and I went to the scheduled meeting place to find Mark Cuban. He wasn't where he said he would be. I left Cena to take a walk down the hall and look for Cuban, and I specifically told Cena not to do anything stupid. No sooner did I leave him, that blockhead bumped into Cuban.

"Stay out of my way, dork! We've got a big meeting here in a few minutes with a billionaire!"

I found Cuban and brought him back into the room, completely unaware that the two had already met. Cena was quick to switch gears, trying to make amends for his earlier blunder, but that went out the window when Cuban said, "I thought you were bringing me Leviathan!"

Leviathan, who became Batista when he went to the WWE, was not a member of Bolin Services but a disciple of Synn, one of my rivals at OVW and Jim Cornette's now wife. Once Cuban brought up Leviathan, Cena was absolutely impossible.

I did everything I could to salvage the meeting. I reminded both men that this was about business. "We don't have to like each other. We just have to work together." At the end of the day, I truly thought we had a deal. I left Indianapolis with a video tape of the encounter and a smile on my face.

No sooner did we arrive home, word leaked out about my little meeting with Mark Cuban. They'll all deny it now, but Danny Davis, Jim Cornette, and Vince McMahon were all scared to death. I know for a fact Vince was scared because one night, I got a phone call at 3 AM from Jimmy.

"What the hell is all this I'm hearing about you and Mark Cuban?" he said.

"I don't know, Jimmy," I said, "What are you hearing?"

"I'll tell you who I'm hearing from," he said. "Vince McMahon just called me. He's pissing his pants that you and Cuban are planning to take over not just OVW but the WWE! What have you done? What are you going to do?"

I laughed, and called back a phrase Jim had once said to me. "Watch for the sharpshooter, Jim. Watch for the sharpshooter."

Anonymous WWE Executive

For many years Vince listened to the tales that Jim Cornette would tell about his childhood friend, Kenny Bolin. Jim would go on an on about his buddy who was obsessed with wrestling, who always had a "get rich quick" money scheme going on. Vince laughed, but he never believed Kenny Bolin existed. He was certain Kenny was Jim's childhood imaginary friend. Having been raised most of his life by his beloved mother, and it made sense that Jim would invent a funny, like-minded best pal to share his boyhood.

Then one night, during a show in Louisville, Vince met Kenny Bolin in person. "Meeting Kenny was surreal," he said. "It was sort of like meeting the Easter Bunny. After meeting him, I wished to God it had never happened. Honestly and truly, I wish I could convince myself he was imaginary. But I can't. He's real. I can't tell you how much it haunts me."

Kenny

Unfortunately, for reasons that still confound me, the deal with Mark Cuban never materialized. He never invested a dime in Bolin Services, and once again I became a laughingstock. That son of a bitch Cornette even aired the videotape just to rub it in.

Cuban went on to become a reality star. Cena went on to become the face of the WWE. I can't help but think how much higher all three of us could have soared if that jackass hadn't called Mark Cuban a dork!

I still keep in touch with Cuban, and he does the same. Cuban never made a play for the WWE, but he does own the parent company of Ring of Honor. A few years back he called asking my advice for the promotion.

"I'm looking for a new executive director at Ring of Honor," he said.

153

"Mark, I'm flattered," I replied, "But my in-ring days are over, and I'm happy with the work I am doing."

"If you were available, the job would be yours," he said. "I was actually calling for a reference on one of the applicants. What can you tell me about Jim Cornette?"

I nearly choked.

"Well, Mark," I said, "You can hire him, but he'll just recycle the same tired shit he did at Smokey Mountain Wrestling and OVW. And mark my words, one day, you'll end up firing him."

Mark thanked me for my input and hired Jim anyway. He lasted a few years and sure enough, he was fired, just like he was from every other wrestling job he ever had. Sorry, Mark, I tried to warn you!

Terry Garvin Simms

Who else but Kenny Bolin could have convinced a billionaire like Mark Cuban to appear on television for a small, local wrestling promotion?

Mark Cuban

Kenny is truly a star maker. If only he would burn the videos he has of me and Cena way, way back when we were both in the rise. But then if it weren't for Kenny, no one would care about those videos. Congrats, Kenny.

IN THE KING'S COURT: LIFE IN BOLIN SERVICES

As the leader of Bolin Services, it became my life's work to pour my years of wrestling knowledge and experience into the men who trusted their careers into my hands. I took my responsibilities as a mentor, a coach, and yes, a friend, very seriously.

I didn't just open my business to these boys. I opened my home. Bolin Manor became a gathering place for members of Bolin Services and other OVW students who, quite frankly, weren't satisfied with the teaching Jim Cornette offered them alone. My house became a safe place to relax, talk about wrestling, and enjoy a good meal.

Sylvester Terkay

Everyone in Bolin Services had their role. I was "The Collector," and it was my job to collect what was owed to Mr. Bolin. It wasn't near as glamorous as it appears in the Godfather movies. Kenny would call me up and invite me over to watch Raw. When I accepted, he'd tell me to drop by some pizza place and get food.

When I arrived at the restaurant, the pizza was hot and ready. I'd pick it up and walk out, with no money ever being exchanged. I drove all over Louisville picking up food for Kenny. I had to get one thing at one place and another at this other place in order to get in the door. Not once did I pay a dime for anything.

Kenny made a lifestyle out of getting free meals. Steak N Shake, Golden Corral, Mr. Gatti's Pizza, Hooters. You name it, Kenny knows a guy, and he can get it for free. If not for free, in exchange for a few DVD movies. Sure, they have Chinese subtitles, but the quality is still excellent.

I will say this about my time with Bolin Services. When I was there, I was never hungry. In fact, I probably gained a few pounds while I was at OVW.

Kenny was a master at bartering. When the air conditioning went out in his car, he was able to get an eight hundred dollar repair job without paying a dime. He could get about anything he wanted with wrestling tickets and a few Steak and Shake gift certificates.

Nova/Simon Dean, former ECW/WWE star

No one bothered to smarten me up to the Kenny Bolin ways when I first arrived at OVW. One night, Kenny took me out to dinner. At the end of the meal, the waitress brought our check. Kenny reached into his bag and pulled out a stack of autographed photos of himself. I asked him what he was doing, and he told me he was paying for the meal!

"Don't worry, I've got you covered too," he said. He reached back in the bag and pulled out a signed photo of me!!

When my now ex-wife came to Louisville for the first time, Kenny took us out to dinner. Afterwards, he invited us back to the house to play ping pong and watch - I kid you not - The Best of Bolin on DVD. Four hour later, we finally went home. I had never seen anyone get blown up playing ping pong until that night. But yes, he did beat me more than I beat him.

Rico Costantino

Kenny took me to Kingfish Restaurant in Jeffersonville, Indiana one night for my birthday. We had a very nice dinner and a great night, but things took a turn when the bill for $100 arrived. "I don't want to pay this!" said Kenny. "I don't suppose you could chip in a little, could you?"

"Me?" I said. "This is my birthday! You said you were taking me out."

Kenny nodded. "Wait here," he said. He goes over and begins to talk to the waitress. I can't hear what they are saying, but I see he keeps pointing over at me. Finally, the two of them walked back over to the table.

"This young lady has agreed to knock some of our bill off, if you will give her a kiss," said Kenny.

I couldn't believe what I was hearing, but I figured why not? I stood up and gave her my best. I laid one of those hot Italian kisses on her and figured we'd see what happened.

A few minutes later, the girl came back to our table and told us the meal was free. An $100 dinner, paid for by a kiss! I couldn't believe it.

Jerry Jarrett

Kenny is one of the most creative minds in the wrestling business, and not just in the ring. One night when I was in Louisville, Kenny called me up and said, "Let me buy you dinner." Well, when I got to the restaurant, I found out that Kenny had already arranged for us to eat for free by telling the manager that he was bringing me to the restaurant. The manager of the restaurant comped a hundred dollar tab and thanked Kenny for the privilege of doing it! I've never seen anything like it in my life.

Aron "The Idol Stevens, aka Damien Sandow

I was Kenny's roommate for almost a year, and it was one of the best years of my life because a hardly ever had to pay for a meal. We ate out all the time, at Golden Corral, Steak and Shake, Applebees, you name it, and we ate for free. At one point we decided to make it a challenge and see how long we could go without paying for a meal. We went fourteen days, two whole weeks, ate out ever meal, never paid a dime.

Rico Costantino

Kenny is the greatest negotiator I have ever seen. He could sell ice to an eskimo. When I went back into law enforcement, I took what I learned from Kenny and applied it to my job. Now, when I give a ticket to someone or even book someone in jail, I do it like Kenny would, and they thank me for it.

Kenny

A man my size has to eat, and yes, I do have my preferred spots in Louisville where the King has special relationships with management and wait staff. I realize most people and businesses still deal in cold, hard cash, but if someone is willing to work on the barter system, then that's the man I want to deal with.

At any rate, another plus sized manager has me beat when it comes to getting something for nothing. OVW booked a show at the casino boat in

Rising Sun, Indiana, and on this occasion, the late Paul Bearer was along for the ride. We stayed in the hotel the night after the show, and we were all given coupons for a free breakfast buffet.

The next morning, I woke up late and had a very nice breakfast with Paul Bearer, Kane, Bobby Eaton, and a few others. We were supposed to be out of the hotel and on our way to our next shows by noon, but none of us had to be anywhere until late that evening and none of us were known for being on time. So when the wait staff changed over to lunch right about noon, Paul Bearer went up and got himself a big plate of fried chicken.

I figured if Paul Bearer could do it, why couldn't I? So I went up and helped myself to some lunch. So did Kane, Bobby, and the rest of our group. We stayed there shooting the breeze all afternoon, and you guessed it, around 5:30 we had a nice dinner before finally leaving the hotel.

The group of us ate three meals - breakfast, lunch, and dinner - on one free breakfast coupon. I am told that OVW was never invited back to the casino because of it.

Chris Bolin

Growing up around wrestlers was never a big deal to me. It was only when I got a glimpse of my life through the eyes of others that I realized how cool it was. In my mind went home after school, did homework, and played video games with Mike Bucci. In the eyes of others, I was the lucky kid who went home and played games with Hollywood Nova of the Blue World Order.

The guys treated me well, but being the King's son didn't mean I had free reign. One night some of the guys were over watching a movie. We discovered that a certain wrestler (whom I will not name) had a certain fear (that I also will not name). He was so afraid of said thing that he couldn't even see it on TV. I started to taunt him, calling him a crying little girl. He responded by getting up, walking over and sitting on top of me.

I was fifteen years old, scared to death, unable to do a thing. I was completely at the mercy of this enormous man now screaming in my face, "Who's the scared little girl now, huh???" After what felt like an eternity, he got up. Needless to say I was much more cautious about teasing him from then on!

Kenny

After John Cena left me and left OVW for the big time, more of my clients began to follow. Losing guys like Sean O'Haire, Mark Henry, and Rico Costantino might have been a blow to a lesser manager, but not to me. The more clients I lost to the WWE, the more people I had beating down the doors of Bolin Manor begging for a chance to be next. Rob Conway, the future WWE Tag Team Champion and two time NWA World Champion, actually signed with me three times. He kept quitting on me, but every time he did, he realized the error of his ways and came crawling back.

I remember going to Applebee's one night for dinner and requesting my usual table in April's section. April was a bright aspiring model from Shepherdsville, Indiana who waited tables by day and did photo shoots by night. I liked April so much, I did a mature but very tasteful photo shoot with her myself.

On this particular night I was stunned when a large, hulking man with a striking look appeared at our table side.

"You're not April," I said.

"P-p-please, Mr. Bolin," said the man wearing April's too small shirt and name tag. "I want to be in the WWE, and I know you are the man who can get me there."

"You didn't hurt April, did you?" I said.

"No, sir!" he said. "I paid her five hundred bucks to let me take her section."

I liked the boy's dedication, so right there in Applebee's, I signed a contract with Gene Snitsky.

I like to think I did pretty well with the signings I made as head of Bolin Services. Our record speaks for itself. Thirty-seven titles were held during the time I ran Bolin Services, and nearly everyone who worked for me at least got a chance to be in the WWE.

Even after all my success, Cornette wouldn't give me any credit. He said it was the talent, not my skills as a manager, that propelled my clients to stardom. After a number of call ups, I brought in Lance Cade and Mark Jindrak, two guys Cornette had rejected. When Jimmy found out I had signed his cast offs, he called me up, laughing.

"You really think you can walk on water, don't you?" he said.

"No, Jimmy, I don't," I said. "But so far, I'm doing better at sending talent to the WWE than you. I haven't missed a one yet."

"You're about to miss two in a row," said Jim. "There's no way either of those two will see a day in the WWE!"

Like he is so many times, Cornette was wrong about my boys!

Shortly after Cade and Jindrak left, Cornette gave me a new nickname, a moniker I bear proudly to this day: the Starmaker. During a TV taping, Cornette called me into the ring to give him his due.

"Well if it isn't the old Starmaker," Cornette said in greeting.

I ignored his false niceties and put Jimmy right in his place. "You told me Cade and Jindrak would never make it to the WWE! I told you I'd get them to the WWE, and you looked at me like I had a smoking turd in my mouth!"

I am proud to say that on that occasion, I became the only man to ever make Jim Cornette break up and laugh on television.

Sylvester Terkay

I was in Japan, getting ready to work a show. This was while I was still doing shows with OVW but before my call up to WWE. I was looking out on the Pacific Ocean with Nova and Paul London, and the three of us got to talking. I don't remember who brought up the name, but somehow the three of us ended up discussing Kenny Bolin.

"Do you guys know Kenny Bolin?" asked London.

Nova laughed. "I feuded with him and Cena a few years back at OVW!"

"Really?" I said. "I'm working for him now. He's my manager at OVW."

London laughed. "I'm headed to OVW in a few weeks. I've heard stories."

We shared a few more stories with Paul. Strange that in such a beautiful country, gazing out at the wonder that is the Pacific Ocean, three guys who barely knew one another found a common connection thanks to Kenny Bolin.

My apologies to those of you who only like funny Kenny who makes you laugh. I have to take a moment to remember a few gentlemen who were taken from us too soon.

It is said a father should never outlive his son. I'd like to add that a manager should not outlive his wrestlers, especially when those wrestlers become more than clients. The boys who came through Bolin Services were like sons to me, every one of them. Losing Lance Cade and Sean O'Haire broke my heart.

Lance Cade was never supposed to make it to the WWE. Cornette didn't believe in him, and neither did anyone else on staff at OVW. But the Starmaker had a way of bringing out the best in everyone he managed. Cade and his tag partner Jindrak got the call up in 2003, and Cade spent nearly five years on the WWE roster. He became a three time Tag Team Champion with Trevor Murdoch.

Here, in his own words, is what Cade once said on a podcast about his time in Bolin Services.

Lance Cade

You got a real education working for Bolin Services, and I don't just mean in the ring. I didn't know who Foghorn Leghorn was until I worked for Kenny. One time Paul Heyman tried to teach Kenny how to do a promo, as if Kenny needed help. Paul went into this weird, Southern sounding voice and stammered his way through the promo. Heyman walked off, and Bolin turned to us. "Do I really sound like that?"

"You kind of do, boss," we said.

"Really?" he said. "I sound like Foghorn Leghorn?"

"Who's Foghorn Leghorn?" I asked.

Kenny was beside himself, but in his fatherly, compassionate way, he put his arm around me. "I'll show you who Foghorn Leghorn is. Pick up a couple pizzas after practice and come by the house. I'll waive the cover charge." That was Kenny. Always generous, and always the good teacher.

Kenny

Lance was born in Carroll, Iowa on March 2, 1981. He trained under Shawn Michaels and worked at Heartland Wrestling Association in Cincinnati before coming to OVW. He passed away August 13, 2010 at the age of 29. Like many of my wrestler, he always called me Dad, and I loved him like a son.

Sean O'Haire worked for WCW and WWE before becoming a part of Bolin Services. He even held the WCW tag titles with Chuck Palumbo prior to coming to the WWE, where he and his fellow WCW stars were more or less squashed in the failed Invasion storyline.

O'Haire had a great look and physique, and so much passion for what he did. His experience was invaluable to the other members of Bolin Services. He was the seasoned veteran of the group, and he taught the boys a great deal.

Early in his OVW career, I paired Cena with O'Haire as a tag team. Cena had a bit of the starry-eyed wrestling fan in him in the early days, and with an endless stream of wrestling legends walking through our door, he could be as star-struck as anyone. One night at Six Flags, he and Sean were matched against OVW trainee David Flair and his father, a fella I mentioned earlier in this book by the name of Ric. Soon as we reached our corner, Cena looked me in the eyes, pointed to the ramp, and said, "Do you see what we are about to do? We're gonna wrestle Ric fuckin' Flair!"

I replied with a big smile, "Yes, boys, yes you are."

Sean looked at Cena as serious as all get out. "Snap out of it you starry eyed mark!" he said. "We gotta JOB to do!" Sean made put our right hands together and yell, "GO BS!!!" Cena could not wipe the smile off his face after that.

Sean was born February 25, 1971 in Hilton Head Island, South Carolina. He passed away September 8, 2014. He was as intense and serious a performer as I ever had the privilege of managing. I miss him dearly.

THE BETRAYAL OF MA BOLIN, AND OTHER MEMORABLE MATCHES

For many people, wrestling is a family affair. The wrestling industry is full of second and third generation wrestlers, referees, and promoters. Stephanie McMahon, for example, is a third generation executive, having followed her father and grandfather into the business. Randy Orton is also a third generation star. The Usos are the sons of Rikishi. Goldust and Stardust are the sons of the late Dusty Rhodes. Bray Wyatt and Bo Dallas are the sons of Mike Rotunda, aka Irwin R. Shyster. Between Dusty's boys and Rotunda's boys, I'm not sure which one would be the creepier place to spend the holidays.

When it came time for me to put up the briefcase and retire from management, my son Christopher, aka the Prince was ready and waiting to take it up. In doing so, Christopher became the first third generation manager in the history of professional wrestling. That's right, third generation.

"Wait a minute, Mr. Bolin, you said your father wasn't into wrestling, and I don't recall reading that your mother was into wrestling either."

True, observant reader, neither my mother nor my father preceded me in the world of professional wrestling. However, Ma Bolin did follow me into the business, making her grandson the first third generation manager in the process. It's all thanks to my childhood hero, that son of a gun from Memphis, Jerry "The King" Lawler.

The King was once my friend, a friendship forged by a mutual love for wrestling and a mutual dislike for one of the favorite past times of pro wrestlers, drinking. One time I met a fan who claimed to have been friends with Lawler just as I was. When I asked him to elaborate, he told me he and Lawler used to meet up at a bar after the Tuesday shows to drink. I told him that was impossible and he was a liar because Jerry Lawler's never drunk a drop of alcohol in his life!

I don't know what I said or did to make the King turn on me, but one summer, the King came down from the WWE to face Charles "The Hammer" Evans during our Six Flags Summer Sizzlin' series. Ma Bolin was there that night sitting ringside, and to add insult to injury, she came to root for Jerry instead of her own son. I was so furious, I had her banned, not just from the arena, but from Six Flags!

Jerry was only supposed to work one night, but when that son of a gun saw what happened with Ma Bolin, he canceled his flight to come back the next night. This time he was set to face Jacob Duncan with the stipulation that if he won, he got five minutes with me in the ring. As if he stood a chance!

Everything seemed to be business as usual that evening. My boys and I made our way to the ring and waited for the King to arrive. He stepped out from the curtain with a microphone and addressed the crowd.

"I have a special guest manager," he said. "She's the woman Kenny Bolin had thrown out of here last night, the same woman he got evicted because he refused to pay her mortgage!"

I couldn't believe what I was hearing. It wasn't possible. It was Ma Bolin's Bingo night, and there's no way anyone or anything would keep her from Bingo!

"Last night, Kenny Bolin had his own mother kicked out of Kentucky Kingdom. Tonight, she is coming to the ring as my guest manager. Ma Bolin!!!"

Ma Bolin

I was getting ready to go to Bingo when the phone rang that night. If I hadn't met him before many times and known his voice, I'd have thought it was a prank. "Hello, Ma Bolin?" he said. "This is Jerry Lawler. I have a favor to ask."

"What's that?" I said.

"I need you to come to Kentucky Kingdom and be my manager tonight," he said.

"I'm sorry, Mr. Lawler," I replied. "It's my Bingo night."

"Ma Bolin, please!" said Jerry. "Come to Kentucky Kingdom. Be my manager tonight. Let's teach Kenny a lesson he's had coming for a long time."

"It's Bingo," I said again.

"How about you bring some of your girls with you?" he said. Finally, I agreed to go.

Kenny

When I saw my own mother walk through that curtain, my jaw dropped. It couldn't be! It was Bingo night, and the old bat never missed Bingo.

It was also illegal. The state of Kentucky required anyone who crosses the barrier wall between the fans and the ring to have a license. That includes ring announcers, time keepers, and yes, even managers. I was ready to lodge a protest, but the athletic commissioner was no where in sight, and neither were Danny Davis or Jim Cornette. Somehow I knew that it was not a coincidence those two were absent.

Ma Bolin got the biggest pop of the night as she walked the aisle and took her seat beside the ring, which just goes to show you how ignorant today's fans are. Then they really went wild when Lawler went after me. He got me all tangled up in the ropes and brought my mother up to the ring.

"Slap him!" said Lawler. "Slap him for every evil thing he ever did in his life!"

My mother hesitated. I knew she was looking at me as her little angel, her sweet baby who didn't deserve this treatment from a former friend and his own mother. Lawler kept on hounding her and hounding her. Finally, she gave me a little tap on the cheek.

"Hit him again!" Lawler shouted. "Come on, Ma Bolin, you know all the terrible things your baby boy did! Hit him again!"

Ring and TV announcer Dean Hill leapt into the fray and joined in. "Come on, Ma Bolin, slap him!"

As I looked at my mother, I began to see a change in her eyes. It was as if I could see scenes from my past flashing through her eyes. The day I shut her any my sister out of my room with the warm heater, refusing to give anyone but my sister's child shelter from the cold. The day I cut off her power and grocery allowance for failure to pay her rent. The day she discovered the hole in the wall I made with my sister's head. Ma Bolin hauled off and bitch slapped me like a woman gone berserk. She hit me again and again and again!

Despite the egregious abuse on the part of both Lawler and Ma Bolin, it was Bolin Services that got the win via disqualification when Lawler tried to hit me with a pile driver. I wasn't in the mood to celebrate at first. It's not every day your mother teams with your childhood idol to humiliate you. But as I thought back on that day, I realized what it meant. Not only did I become a second generation manager, I defeated Jerry "The King" Lawler, a former USWA and AWA champion!

Jerry Lawler

Kenny Bolin is probably responsible for one of my all time favorite jokes. Of course the fans are not crazy about Kenny so they call him all kinds of names. I said, "Kenny Bolin doesn't care what you call him, so long as you don't call him late for dinner."

Let's face it Kenny is a big guy! I mean I think the nickname Starmaker came because he's so big, he has his own gravitational pull.

Kenny and I go back a long way. I remember him telling me stories of him as a child and Jimmy Cornette sitting around the house, (and when Kenny sits around the house, he sits AROUND the house) watching me and Bill Dundee on Saturday morning wrestling, wanting the show to hurry up and be over so they could go out into the backyard and pretend to be me and Dundee.

I like to think that Kenny Bolin got his entire persona from the heel Jerry "The King" Lawler. I've had a lot of fun working with Kenny over the years, except the time I actually tried to pick him up for a piledriver. Biggest mistake I ever made! I'm glad he's finally having his entire career put into a book. When it's finished he will have to get somebody to read it to him. I love ya Kenny!

John Cosper

Lawler's not joking. I spent nine months compiling stories and quotes for this book, sending regular updates to Kenny so he could approve them and check the facts. Kenny hasn't read a single page. I could write just about anything I want in this book and he'd never know, which is why I've decided to reveal that Kenny was responsible for the demise of the territories, the divorce of Randy Savage and Miss Elizabeth, and the death of Katie Vick.

Kenny

I'm proud to say that Lawler wasn't the only world champion I defeated one on one in the ring. As I mentioned already, I have a victory over one of the WWE's greatest champions, John Cena. I also have a victory over Rob Conway, another Bolin Services client who is now a two time NWA champion.

Dean Hill, "The Voice of OVW"

There have been many great bumps taken in the history of professional wrestling. One of the greatest bumps every filmed happened the night Mick Foley, whom we all knew from his early days as Cactus Jack, was tossed off the top of a steel cage through an announcer's table by the Undertaker, the man we called Master of Pain in USWA.

As great as that bump was, the greatest bump I know of took place away from the cameras, and only two people witnessed it. It took place on a six foot tall platform, just outside the curtains where we were preparing to do a show. Only four people were present for this historic occasion: Kenny Bolin, Jim Cornette, Danny Davis' daughter April, and myself.

It began when Kenny latched his hands around Jim Cornette's neck to choke him. I can't remember the reason why, but acting on decades of instinct as a member of the Louisville Metropolitan Police Department, I intervened by putting a hold on Mr. Bolin from behind. I was able to get Kenny to let go of Mr. Cornette, but as soon as he did, the weight shifted between us and back we fell, six feet to the concrete floor. I landed first. Kenny landed on top of me.

Kenny

As soon as I landed, I knew Dean was dead. It wasn't even a question in my mind. So you can imagine my surprise when I heard that legendary announcer's voice saying, "Are you okay, King?"

I don't know how he survived that fall, or me falling on top of him. All I can say is those years as a Louisville police officer made Dean Hill one tough son of a gun!

I took one other huge bump during my days with OVW. It was during a coal miner's glove match between Rico Costantino and Rob Conway. I was managing Conway that night, and when Conway was out of the ring, knocked out, I climbed to the top turnbuckle and attempted to climb the pole to reach the coal miner's glove that was suspended on top of the pole. Rico climbed up next to me and pushed me from the top rope. I fell with a mighty crash, and Jim Cornette on commentary said, "The world just got knocked off its axis!"

Dean Hill

I remember watching Kenny drop and do twenty push ups on a bet, just to show he could do them. He did it with hardly any strain or effort. He was an athlete in his younger years, and he still has that athleticism in him.

Rico Costantino

Most people just see a big, fat guy when they see Kenny, but he is by far the most solid big man I have ever known. He can shoot the lights out on a basketball court.

Kenny

When the WWE started sending stars down to work our summer shows at Six Flags Kentucky Kingdom, I made a habit of winning some of that WWE cash off the stars by challenging them to three point shooting contests. The only guy I didn't beat was Chris Jericho, not because he beat me, but he refused to take the challenge. Bobby Lashley and Linda Miles smartened him up before he got there, and he knew better than to accept the King's challenge!

Bill Apter, Legendary Wrestling Journalist

Kenny may be a fine basketball player, but my dream date is to go "bolin" with him one night.

Kenny

We had some good times at Six Flags Kentucky Kingdom. One night after the show, Jim Kunau, the director of the park, told all the boys in the back that Mini B and myself had, quote, "taught everyone on that card how to perform and how to entertain the Six Flags fans." He went on to say that we had performed the best match at Six Flags that year. You should have seen the looks on the boys' faces as Jim told those WWE hopefuls that two non-wrestlers had performed the match of the year his paying audience!

Jim Kunau, Six Flags Kentucky Kingdom

We are in the entertainment industry, wrestlers and theme parks. It's not about who wins or losses but who provides us with the returning, paying guest. That's who I need show after show. Kenny brought it week in and week out.

I have never enjoyed myself so much as calling Kenny out at his weekly taping from across the room. And to have him banter with me made my day. He is an entertainer!

JIM GETS MARRIED AGAIN

On October 31, 2007, Halloween night, Jim Cornette got married. This was not the first marriage for Jim. Not by a long shot. It was actually his fifth wedding. I had been there for the previous four, and I nearly missed the fifth. Lucky for Jimmy, I did not miss that evening because before the night was over, I single-handedly saved the day.

Halloween happened to fall on a Wednesday night that year, the same night that OVW held its weekly television taping. I had not missed a single TV taping, not one, in twelve years, but I knew Jimmy would want his old pal there, so I made arrangements with Danny Davis to be off that night.

This was before I received an invitation, something I believed would be forthcoming since, again, we were old childhood friends. The wedding date was drawing close, so I placed a call to my old buddy and let him know I had not yet seen an invitation.

"I'm sorry, Kenny," said Jim. "It must have gotten lost in the mail."

"Jimmy," I said, "If you want to have people come to your wedding and bring gifts, you need to send invitations,"

"Well, Kenny," he replied, "I know it's Wednesday night, and you have your highly rated wrestling program to tape. I understand if you can't make it."

"No, Jimmy, I've got it covered," I said. "Dean Hill can pull one week without me. They'll get Al Snow or somebody to fill in. I'll be there. I won't let you down."

After Jimmy said okay and the two of us hung up, I realized Jimmy had forgotten to tell me where the wedding was. I called him back and told him I needed to know where the big event would be if he wanted me around.

Jimmy hemmed and hawed around, saying again that he didn't want me to have to take off television for the wedding. I told him it was very kind of him to say so, but I insisted I would be there. I'd been the best man at his four previous weddings, and I wasn't going to miss this one. He mentioned a chicken place in Shelbyville, and we hung up once more.

After a little research and process of elimination, I figured out they would be at Claudia Sanders' restaurant. Claudia was the second wife of Col. Sanders, and her place was one of the Colonel's former homes, a beautiful old mansion that had been made over into a restaurant.

I headed out in my sedan the night of the wedding for Shelbyville. For some reason, everyone seemed surprised to see me.

"Jim said you'd be busy with OVW," said one guest.

"I have no idea you would be here," said another.

"Why wouldn't I be here?" I said. "I'm Jimmy's best friend. I was the best man at his last wedding, and the one before, and the two before that!"

177

Finally, I got to Jimmy. Even he looked shocked and surprised to see me. Nevertheless, Jimmy escorted me to the seat, a special place he said, way in the back of the room. "Just sit here, Kenny," he said. "And if I need you, I'll give you a holler."

My seat go honor was close to the buffet, so I decided to sample some of the fare. For some reason, Jimmy didn't want Claudia Sanders' food, and he'd had a bunch of other stuff catered in. There was some prime rib and a few sirloin steaks, but nothing truly spectacular. Believe me, I sampled them all, and I really wasn't impressed.

I decided I better tell Jimmy that the buffet was a bust and make the recommendation that we can in an order from some place else. Either that, or we needed to get Claudia in the kitchen to whip up some fried chicken for us because the fare Jimmy paid for was just no good.

Unfortunately, it turned out that it was too late to get any replacement food, which was sad. Many of the guests ended up not even eating. They tried to be polite and told Jimmy that some heartless fat ass had eaten their portion before they could, but I knew the truth.

My pursuit of a new chef to save the wedding dinner was cut off when the music started and the ceremony begin. This caught me by surprise, especially when Jimmy appeared up front and Stacy made her entrance, walking down the aisle. I knew then and there Jimmy had to be extremely nervous because he completely forgot to grab his best man on the way up to the ceremony. Jimmy had some 150 pound weakling by his side who was obviously a stand-in for the best man because who else but me was supposed to be the best man?

I went up there to take my place and wouldn't you know it, the little punk wouldn't step down! I said, "Listen, kid I'm the best man. I don't know who you are or who you think you are, but I'm the King! I took Wednesday night TV taping off to be here, and if you don't step aside, you're going to ruin my best friend's wedding!"

I looked over at Jimmy, who clearly looked befuddled by the situation. Who could blame him? Some punk was ruining this special moment by not allowing his best man to take his place. Jimmy pulled the guy aside and talked to him. I saw some money change hands, and the punk went and sat down.

The wedding ceremony itself was pretty strange. They had a female minister performing a very Halloween-themed wedding. There was some witchcraft, some spells were spoken, and hell, a few people nearly got set on fire.

I don't know where this preacher woman got her training, but I quickly realized she was misquoting the Bible. So I did the right thing and started to correct her every time she got something wrong. I felt so bad for Jim and Stacy having hired this numbskull to officiate their special day, but with a little help from me, she got back on course, and the ceremony went on.

By this point, I was feeling pretty proud of myself. I had taken TV off to be there for my best friend. I surprised Jimmy by even being there. I had done Jim and his guests a huge favor in finding all the bad food on the buffet. I had gotten rid of the punk who thought he was going to be Jim Cornette's best man, and I had made sure the wedding was conducted in a proper, Christian fashion. In a nutshell, I saved Jim and Stacy's wedding.

I was so moved by the moment, I felt like I needed to say something as the best man. I grabbed a microphone and gave a long speech. I shared some stories about Jimmy, spoke about his previous four weddings and how none of them had panned out so well, and I expressed my hopes that he and Stacy would make it work.

Well, after the vows were said, something awkward happened. As you know, it is tradition that at the conclusion to the ceremony, the best man gets to kiss the bride. Now I knew going in that Stacy had a thing for me, and truth be told, she probably would have preferred to marry me instead of Jimmy. It occurred to me as I went in for that kiss that this would probably be the last time in her life Stacy would be on the receiving end of a really good kiss. I've seen Jimmy kiss before, and believe me, he leaves a lot to be desired in the romance department. I decided to give Stacy a little something to remember, so I slipped her a little tongue.

That's when things got a little awkward. I knew she was liking this, but as soon as my tongue went in her mouth, she started kicking and biting and hitting me, putting on a good show for Jimmy so he wouldn't realize how much she liked it. Jimmy starts to get all hot about it, and he started saying things he didn't mean, like he didn't want me at the wedding, much less to be his best man, and he didn't appreciate me saying all those things about his previous weddings.

Next thing I know I'm giving another speech and the place is starting to clear out. I felt kind of sorry for Jimmy when I saw that. Yeah, I know he lost his temper and that probably made everyone mad, but no one should have guests walking out on your wedding day.

But then I looked toward the back and lo and behold, I saw Jimmy sneaking out the door, leaving with his new bride without so much as a goodbye for his best man! I ran to the back door because I knew he had forgotten about me and the good things I was saying about him.

Jim told me they were tired and headed off to the hotel, and he thanked me again for coming. I gave Jimmy a big hug and told thanks weren't necessary. This was all about him, and it had been my pleasure. I had given up a big payday at OVW to be there, and I wasn't looking for any money for my efforts. But then again, it was a long drive to the restaurant, I had gotten lost, and I figured I was owed a little something at least for gas.

Jim and Stacy received quite a bit of cash as gifts that night, so as he stepped into the limo, I reached in and took out a few bucks for transportation, plus a little something to reimburse for missing TV that night. I also took enough to give some back, and when I gave Jim that fifty dollar bill, he really seemed touched. I also slipped a few DVDs into his bag, all autographed of course which upped the value.

I was quite proud of myself at the end of the night, and I know to this day Jimmy is thankful for all I did for him and his new bride. I wish I could say the memories of that day are still fond for me, but for reasons I will disclose in the next chapter, I regret that I didn't stop that wedding and send that horrible woman back where she came from when I had the fucking chance!

HEIR TO THE BOLIN AND CORNETTE FORTUNES

In the summer of 1987 I met the second most remarkable man I ever knew in my life, after myself. That was when my then-wife Gabrielle gave birth to my son in Nashville, Tennessee. Christopher Michael James Bolin was named after two of my childhood friends, Mike Coffey and Jim Cornette.

Now I am not exactly a religious man, but Gabrielle was very religious and insisted on having Chris baptized. I contacted Jimmy and asked him to be there, as I not only wanted to have my best friend present, but name him as Chris's godfather. Jimmy is no religious man either, but my dear friend assured me he would be there, "as long as you book it on a Sunday. Saturdays are busy, but Sundays are good." Only in the wrestling business will you hear someone talk about "booking" a baptism.

The day finally arrived, and much to my shock, Jimmy was a no show. He didn't call, and he didn't make an appearance. I was upset, to say the least! It took me a few days, but I finally got ahold of him.

"That fuckin' Dusty Rhodes," he said, "He booked me on a double shot in Georgia and Virginia. I'm sorry, Kenny, I wanted to be there, but Dusty wouldn't let me come!"

Knowing the wrestling business, I took Jim at his word and accepted his apology.

Flash forward twenty years. I'm standing backstage at Six Flags Kentucky Kingdom with Jim,

Chris, and the American Dream himself, Dusty Rhodes. I'd been around Dusty a few times during the past two decades, but as I finally had Dusty, Jimmy, and Chris in the same place, I decided to air my grievances.

"I have a bone to pick with you, Mr. Rhodes," I said.

"Oh you do?" said Dusty.

I proceeded to tell Dusty the story about Chris's baptism. I told him how we scheduled it specifically so that Jim could be in attendance, and I told him why Jim was unable to attend.

Now, I hate to tell you this, wrestling fans, but the Dusty voice you're used to hearing on TV was not Dusty's natural speaking voice. It's similar, but that's a voice and a character Dusty put on for the crowds. Nevertheless, at that moment, the American Dream went into his signature Dusty voice to answer my grievance.

"No, no, no, Mr. Bolin," he said with that signature lisp and charm. "You got it all wrong. Allow me to tell you the TRUTH, Mr. Bolin. I did not tell Jimmy he could not go to the baptism. Jimmy was given a choice. Jimmy could go to the baptism, or he could get PAID. Jimmy CHOSE to get PAID!"

I looked at Cornette, who was white as a sheet. He nodded and confirmed Dusty's story. It was true. Jimmy chose to get paid. The rat bastard!

I was so sad the day Dusty passed. The Prince and I both had a hard time with the news. Dusty was very gracious any time he joined us at OVW. He was equally gracious with our students. He made it known that if anyone wanted to talk, ask questions, or whatever, Dusty was at their disposal. The sad truth is most of those kids had no idea who Dusty was! It was unreal to me. It would be like Pete Rose walking into a room full of baseball fans and having no one recognize him.

I could go on and on about Dusty, but this chapter's about Christopher and his rightful claim to Jim Cornette's mass fortune.

I've already told you that Chris was the man to step into my shoes when I retired from managing, but Chris' wrestling career began long before that. Chris grew up in the wrestling business. He learned to crawl, walk, and use a toilet inside the locker rooms of wrestling promotions from here to Texas. In his teens he was inside a wrestling ring, learning from the likes of Tony Atlas, Ted DiBiase, Lex Lugar, Tito Santana, and a fella named Stone Cold Steve Austin.

When Bolin Services went into business, young Christopher was just a teenager, yet even he was part of our success. Christopher imparted his own youthful knowledge on all my clients, not the least of which was that ingrate, John Cena.

Yes, my son taught John Cena thing or two about wrestling. Ponder that for a moment!

The Prince, as he is rightly addressed, is a lot like his old man, finding good fortune and success everywhere he goes. He was barely out of high school when he got a job with Central States Hospital in Kentucky, and he went on to become one of the most sought after names in Kentucky law enforcement.

Jim Cornette

Let me tell you the truth about Catbox. First of all, I gave him the name Catbox because when he was nine years old, his father started charging him rent to sleep in the basement beside the cat box. Catbox not only had to pay to stay in his own house at a tender young age, he also had to empty the cat box when dirty.

Regarding the career "success" of the Prince, Kenny once again isn't telling the full truth. Central States is the mental hospital, and Catbox was nothing more than hired muscle, used to hold down patience who didn't want to take their meds.

Kenny charged rent to his own dear mother Ma Bolin as well. Fortunately for her, she was not required to clean out the cat box, but when she fell a month behind on payments one winter, Kenny shipped her off to his sister's house so he could bring in a wrester willing to pay an even higher rent!

As for Catbox being sought after by Kentucky State Law Enforcement, Kenny is partly accurate on that one. Chris has had so many speeding violations and dodged driver safety school so often, he's wanted by the Kentucky State Police, the Louisville Metro Police, the Jefferson County Sheriff's Department, and at least two other local counties that I know of.

Kenny

Christopher's birth was not only an important moment for the Bolin family, but the Cornette family. Jimmy has been married five times, and at the time of Chris' birth, he was on wife two or three. Due to a medical condition that I vowed I would take to the grave, Jimmy has never had children. Jim was so honored that I named him as Christopher's godfather, he vowed that one day, my son would not only be my heir, but Jimmy's.

Jim, for those who don't know, is quite the wealthy man. His father was am important executive with Louisville's hometown newspapers, the *Courier-Journal* and the now defunct *Louisville Times*. The senior Cornette left his wife and son with a million dollar bank account and a gorgeous, multi-million dollar mansion that he himself built.

Jim picks on me for being cheap, but the old fart is as miserly as I am when it comes to his daddy's money. But what good is a multi-million dollar fortune when you have no heir?

Jim

Yes, I am the godfather to that bastard son of Kenny's, but I'm hardly the only god-relative that kid has. Dennis Corralluzzo is the kid's god-uncle. He has god-aunts, god-cousins, godmothers, god-grandparents. Kenny named countless people Catbox's god-relatives, all in the hopes of getting some cash out of them. Not for Catbox, but for Kenny. Don't think for a second all his rantings about Catbox's "inheritance" has anything to do with the welfare of his child!

Kenny

I always knew that one day, Chris would be the one living in Castle Cornette out in Prospect. Chris would be the one living off the media fortune Jim's father left to him. Yes, I'd probably be living comfortably with him, but that's not because I am greedy. Jim told me at an early age that no Cornette male ever lived past the age of 53. Since Bolins have a longer life expectancy than Cornettes by decades, simple math will tell you that I'd be around to see my son enjoy the fruits of his godfather's labor.

Then Cornette met that woman.

OVW fans knew her as Synn, the woman who used evil magic to draw Leviathan/Batista from the waters of the Ohio River. I know her as Stacy. Stacy is a home wrecker who got her mitts into Jim when he was still living up in the Northeast. Jim was married to Kelly, aka wife number four, a very nice and very attractive redhead. Stacy was younger than Kelly by many years. She was also a redhead, but she sure as hell was no Kelly in the attractiveness department.

Once Stacy got her claws into Jim, marriage number four was over. She followed him to Louisville, where he gave her a job - my former job! - as a manager. Jimmy even gave her the pick of the WWE signees. I don't need to tell you that her stable of wrestlers ever equaled the achievements mine did, and I'm including Batista in that assessment.

Jim moved that woman into his father's mansion, where she went right to work spending away Christopher's inheritance. Every day she sits in that mansion, my son's future trust shrinks by at least a couple grand.

It sickens me that this greedy woman would come in to my friend's life and drain him of his father's money. That's not hers to spend. It's Christopher's. He is the rightful heir, and he deserves one hundred percent. True, he's still set to earn half, but by the time she's through with it, he'll end up with half of nothing!

Jim

How much money I have, and to whom I leave that money, is my business. I'm not about to divulge the details of my last will and testament, but I will tell you two things. One, I paid Tim Denison a good chunk of money to write my will so that Kenny cannot contest it. And two, Catbox isn't going to get a dime, a penny, or even a piece of dryer lint from me. Put it this way, if I took a shit in a box before I died and that box of shit ended up in Catbox's hands, I'd rise from the grave to strangle him and his father.

Chris Bolin

Cornette's not gonna leave me a dime? Who gives a fuck? Under US law, I'd only end up with a tiny percentage of it anyway. The house might be nice, but if he wants to leave it to his wife and not his godson, fuck him.

Fuck the government, too, for taxing inheritances so heavily. And while I'm at it, fuck Danny Davis, Trailer Park Trash, Paul Heyman, Vince McMahon, Stephanie McMahon, Triple H, John Laurinitis, Tony Atlas, Lanny Poffo, and especially Rip Rogers.

THE WORST THING I'VE EVER DONE

Some of you may have noticed the name Tim Denison mentioned in this book. You may have wondered, who is Tim Denison, and why should I care?

Mr. Denison is one of the most successful and well respected attorneys in Louisville. As a matter of fact not only is he mine and my son's attorney, he represented Jerry Lawler many times back in the day.

Jim Cornette

Denison got Lawler off. He also did a good job defending him in court!

Kenny

Tim asked to see the manuscript prior to publication to offer his legal counsel. I thought it was a kind gesture, but unnecessary. After all, I am a law abiding citizen with nothing to hide. Nevertheless, Tim read the manuscript and insisted on a few edits and redactions to protect myself and those closest to me from legal action.

I tell you this to explain why a few of the details are blacked out in this chapter, one I've titled "The worst thing I've ever done. I really needed to get this story out to purge my soul, and I appreciate Denison's willingness to step on and protect my best interests.

The story begins when I first ██████████

Hard to believe, but it's true. But that was only the beginning!

The next thing I knew,

191

192

Even now, all these years later, I still wonder what happened to that baby goat.

HOW I BECAME A MEDIA MOGUL

In 2006 I received some bad news from my doctor when I was diagnosed with congestive heart failure. That, coupled with what could be characterized as a little bit of a weight problem, told me the writing was on the wall for my in-ring career. I always knew it couldn't last forever, and rather than hang around past my expiration date like some folks (Hogan, Flair, Cornette), I decided it was time to leave on my own terms.

I spoke to Danny Davis, the owner of OVW, and when Davis learned of my health problems, he begged me not to quit. Danny knew, as did we all, that I was the biggest draw he had, and he feared the worst if I were to leave. I told him I had no intention of continuing to manage, but at Danny's insistence, I took a new position. It was actually my old position because, once again, I would sit at the announcer's desk with Dean Hill.

Many of you Internet fans have seen how great I was in front of the camera, but you may not know what an excellent color commentator I am. I proved my mettle one night after my retirement from management during a Wednesday night TV taping. I arrived early for the pre-show meetings, and went into Danny's office. Danny had a few of the production staff in his office, but when I walked in, he told me to get the hell out.

"Excuse me?" I said. "I'm part of this team, and whatever's going on, I think I should be involved."

"I said get out!" shouted Danny. "Get out, and we'll call you in for the production meeting!"

I went down to the locker room and sat with some of the boys. About ten minutes later Danny sent for me. I told the messenger that I wasn't coming. "Danny insulted me," I said. "If he wants to come out here and apologize, fine, but I'm not going into his meeting."

Danny was furious. By missing the production meeting, I would be going out to do a live TV taping with no show prep and no knowledge of what was happening that night. Danny was content to let me go out there and fall on my face.

I was a bit nervous at first, but I shook those nerves off. It really felt liberating to walk out to the table with Dean Hill and Gilbert Corsey, our Emmy award winning local TV news anchor whom Dean had taken under his wing. Dean and Gilbert knew the show and had notes in front of them, while I sat down with only my years of knowledge and experience.

I thought the show went fine, in my humble opinion, but I fully expected Danny to rip my ass when I walked to the back. I let Dean and Gilbert take the lead, and I was last through the curtain.

Danny was waiting for me, arms folded as I walked into the back. He grabbed me by the lapels and said, "Kenny, that was the best damn show I ever heard. From now on, you don't have to be in any meetings. Show up at five 'til seven if you want. You proved me wrong, and you earned it."

I did earn it, and I took full advantage of Danny's offer. I never made another production meeting.

Al Snow

Kenny is and always has been an ultimate professional in every sense of the word.

Huh... What... We're not talking about Ken Anderson?

Oh .... Uh .... Yeah .... Well ... Um ...

So Kenny Bolins is those things too sort of ......

Just kidding Kenny Starmaker Bolin is untouchable on the mic. Kenny is truly a talented performer who understands the true art of storytelling in professional wrestling on every level.

Kenny knows how to accentuate what the in ring performers are doing and then convey that in a way that makes you naturally root for the good guy and hate the bad guy.

When Kenny finally hangs up the mic it will be professional wrestling's loss.

Christian Skyfire, Independent wrestler and inventor of the Toy Box Death Match

I got to work an anniversary show for OVW, way back in the early days. Ordinarily when I wrestle I put on big, baggy pants to cover up the fact that I don't have an ass. But since this was OVW, I wanted to look professional so I wore spandex. Those shorts wouldn't stay up for anything, and mid way through the match, they were falling off.

When I got to the back, everyone was laughing, and not just because my shorts were falling off. It seems my wardrobe malefaction became the focal point of the commentary, specifically from Kenny. He spent the entire match cracking one joke after another about my lack of an ass and the new ghetto fad I was trying to start with sagging spandex.

A few months after the show I got my VHS copy and heard it for myself. It was pretty funny.

Kenny

I was thrilled to be back on the microphone, and not just because it meant working with the legendary voice of Louisville wrestling. I had a front row seat to the rise of Bolin Services 2.0.

All his life, my son Chris watched his father work in the wrestling business. By the time I was ready to step down, Chris knew more about professional wrestling than 90 percent of the men and women in the WWE, including the McMahon offspring and a certain son-in-law.

Even with not training or in-ring experience, Chris was already a fixture at Davis Arena. He and his friends had long established their power to make and break stars from the stands. Sitting middle center of the Arena, Chris and his crew could get the entire crowd to cheer and boo talent almost at will. When Cornette disputed their power to put stars over, Chris took it as a challenge. The following week, the group refused to give any kind of reaction for one of OVW's lead babyfaces. To Cornette's surprise, the entire crowd went along with the Prince, and the babyface entered to deafening silence.

Bolin Services 2.0 picked right up where the original incarnation left off, and I was proud to watch our legacy grow.

Happy as I was to be behind the announcer's desk, the pay cut from managing meant that I needed to look for some outside sources of income. Once again, I was ready. Over the years, I had amassed a large collection of wrestling videos, thanks to some connections I have throughout the professional wrestling world. In the mid 1990s I beat the WWE to the punch by offering classic wrestling on DVD. My best seller by far was Memphis Classics, a hand-picked assortment of wrestling matches from the last of the great territories. I also released five volumes of AWA footage, and a greatest hits collection of my own, "A Decade of BS."

As I eased into my new life as a video salesman and announcer, many fans reached out to me expressing their appreciation for all my years of work. Many of them remarked that they believed I could have done more than I did. After all, I'm the man responsible for John Cena. I'm the only manager I know who can claim that at one time, the three major world wrestling champions were former clients of his. That's right! In the summer of 2014, John Cena was the WWE champ, Bobby Lashley was the TNA champ, and Rob Conway was the NWA champ, all at the same time!

People continued to ask why I never made it to the big time, to the WWE or even WCW. I realized I had a story to tell, and I needed an outlet to share it.

That outlet was a new form of media called podcasting. Podcasts are like Internet radio shows, shows you can download and listen to at your leisure. These days the most popular wrestling podcasters are guys like Steve Austin, Chris Jericho, and Jim Ross. All of these men were merely riding on my coat tails because by the mid 2000s, I was the first true wrestling star in the podcast in the world. Not Austin, not Jericho, and certainly not Colt Cabana!

I had never done radio before, but I found podcasting to be a snap. I had my own segment called "The Bolin Alley" on a show produced and hosted by Tommy Fiero. I settled into a groove, and I built my show on one agenda: to expose Jimmy Cornette for the lying sack of shit he is. Each week, I would ask people to write in and submit their horror stories of meeting Jim Cornette. Chance encounters while traveling, face to face meetings at the autograph table, and spotting him at a flea market. I revealed shocking story after shocking story, including the true story of the Montreal Screwjob as I told you in an earlier chapter.

The people ate it up, and it didn't take long for Tommy Fiero's ratings to rise. He was drawing thousands of listeners a week to the show, and my segment became the highest rated part of the program, higher than the Iron Shiek, higher even than my hero and mentor, Jerry Jarrett!

Of course Tommy didn't want to give me credit for his success. He told people it was all the marketing he did on social media and other outlets that caused the ratings to climb. That's bullshit, ladies and gentlemen. Tommy Fiero was a success because of me. I was giving the people something they wanted, the whole and unvarnished truth about Jim Cornette. I told how Jim tried to keep me from knowing where his wedding was when he married former OVW manager Synn so I wouldn't show up. I told about Jimmy's flirtations with teenage girls. And so on, and so on.

Most important of all, I was able to tell my millions of fans why I never made it in Memphis, or the NWA, or WCW, or even WWE. It was all because of Jim Cornette. Once Jim got in with Jerry Jarrett, he begged Jarrett to shut me out of the business. True, Jimmy did give me a chance to be a guest ring announcer at Smokey Mountain Wrestling, and he didnt's bar the door when Bolin Services mounted our invasion of OVW, but in both circumstances, Jim was the boss. He only let me in when he could boss me and order me around.

There's only one reason I never made it bigger than I did, and that reason is Jim Cornette.

Jerry Jarrett

I kept a secret for thirty years. I have four cases of Beets by Bolin headphones in my attic that I took as a bribe to continue my silence. But in 2014 I finally had to speak up and clear my conscience.

For thirty years I maintained the lie that it was Jim Cornette who kept Kenny Bolin out of Memphis. Nothing could be further from the truth. Jim begged me to give Kenny a chance, and I did - just once. He was terrible. Kenny stunk the place out! The fans at Louisville Gardens were bringing their tickets from the previous week to the ticket table, demanding their money back from that week's show because Kenny was so awful.

Cornette continued to pester me and pester me to give his old friend a chance. He even got my mother Teeny to lobby on Bolin's behalf. I finally got so sick of hearing Cornette talk about Bolin, I shipped him off to Bill Watts and Mid-South Wrestling, where Jim nearly got killed by the Louisiana fans on a number of occasions.

No, Jim Cornette didn't tell me to keep Kenny Bolin out. I kept Kenny Bolin out because the one time I gave Kenny a shot, he had all the drawing power of a dead jackass!

Kenny

The Bolin Alley grew in popularity, and soon my son Chris joined the show. With Chris by my side the show really went to a new level. Tommy's program was called "Who's Slamming Who," and as Chris and I listened in on our fellow hosts, we realized that no one was really slamming anyone. We went into full on shoot mode and began to speak our minds on everyone from the Iron Sheik to Randy Savage.

Savage's brother Lanny had a show of his own, and Randy did not take kindly to many of the things we said. Lanny tried to keep Randy from responding, but Randy was never the kind of guy to show any restraint. The more Randy responded, the more Chris unloaded on him. We eventually extended an invitation to have Randy join is on the podcast, but before that could happen, Randy passed away.

Tommy Fiero got a lot of complaints from the people Chris and I discussed on our show, and even some fans complained. He tried to tell us to tone things down and asked to edit our shows, but we refused. We knew Tommy was nothing without us, and we had no reason to tone down our discussions. Tommy finally relented, airing our shows unedited with a disclaimer.

The Bolin Alley outlived Who's Slamming Who, becoming a stand alone show in its own right. Seven years later, we are still the most downloaded wrestling podcast on the Internet. Yes, there are people now who draw bigger numbers every week than we did, but our longevity means they have a long way to go.

Cornette is one of the guys out there running his own podcast claiming bigger numbers than mine. However, Jim knows as well as I do his show wouldn't be the hit it is without me. After a year on the air, Jimmy was forced to admit my drawing power. Four of the five top-rated episodes of The Jim Cornette Experience all featured yours truly, and I still question the numbers I was shown on the Rip Rogers episode.

Jimmy knew he needed me if he wanted to grow his ratings, so he was forced to include a little bit of me on each show. The segment is appropriately titled "A Little Bit of Bolin," and wouldn't you know it, it's the most popular segment on the show.

I still record a Bolin Alley episode from time to time, but the demands of my other business enterprises prohibit me from making it a regular gig. For those who wish they could hear more of me, I have good news: all of these shows are available for purchase on one DVD-Rom and can be ordered directly from me if you contact me on Facebook. The Memphis Classics, Bolin Services, and John Cena DVDs are also still available. It's all part of the growing catalog of media goods available from the King, a catalog that now includes my very popular Beets by Bolin headphones.

SPEAKING OF BEETS...

Beets by Bolin, if you're not in the know, are my number one business at the moment and since their introduction have become one of the hottest new accessories for the distinguishing music listener. Contrary to what a certain people may tell you, Beets are not cheap knock offs of the Beats made popular by Dr. Dre. They are engineered from the finest quality materials and designed to deliver superior sound performance. What's more, because I purchase them direct from the factory, Beets can be had at a fraction of the cost of their Dr. Dre inspired cousins.

The idea behind Beets by Bolin began one night at Golden Corral. A sweet woman and her daughter were browsing through my DVD offerings when a young man strolled by wearing a pair of red and black Beats by Dre.

"Mom," said the young girl, "That's what I want for Christmas. I want Beats!"

"No," said her mother. "Those are too expensive and you know it."

Now I have always considered myself a connoisseur of electronics, but I confess I had not looked at Beats by Dre specifically because I preferred a much higher end brand. I asked the woman how much a pair of those Beats would run, and I was shocked at the price. $400 for a pair of fucking headphones!

"But Mom," said little Agatha, "I want some. Everyone at school has them!"

"If I could get you some at a decent price, I would," said the mother.

It was then that a light bulb went off in my head. It had been a while since I'd stumbled upon a new product idea, a real winner. What's more, my stock of signed John Cena 8 x 10 photos was gone, leaving a big hole in my product offerings. I saw an opportunity, and I accepted the challenge.

I took the $19.95 the woman owed me for the John Cena: Our Life DVD and then made the women a promise. "If it is in my power, I will find a way to get little Agatha some great headphones."

After making some phone calls to some friends I know overseas, I stumbled upon a manufacturer making not Beats, but better than Beats headphones. The owner of the factory, who knew me from watching OVW on the Internet, was delighted at the idea of taking on a celebrity endorser, and a deal was struck. Two months later, I received my first shipment of Beets by Bolin, and a few days after they arrived, I sold little Agatha the first pair for only $39.

Beets by Bolin were initially only available in black and white, but as demand grew, so did the color selection. Fans were allowed to customize the logos on the side, and I added new accessories like a microphone cable and my very popular Buds by Bolin earbuds. It's an old-fashioned American business success story.

Jim Cornette

One Saturday night Kenny was getting ready to leave when a bus load of high school kids headed for some sports tournament pulled up outside. Kenny ended up selling thirty pairs of those cheap, Chinese rip off headphones to the coach!

Kenny

Some people can't get over their jealousy. They are jealous of my career, jealous of my success, and jealous of my undeniable ability to see an opportunity and grab it. And for the record, those headphones come from the Philippines, not China!

Beets by Bolin have their own cult-like following, just like Beats by Dre. And thanks to a news story that broke after the 2015 Kentucky Derby, my Beets now have more "street cred" than Dre's.

Shortly after the 141st Run for the Roses, the local and national news channels picked up a story about two men and a young woman who murdered a Canadian man in town to see the Derby. The three had worked out a con in which the woman feigned that she was being mugged. When unsuspecting passersby decided to play Good Samaritan, her two companions would jump the victim and rob them. Things went perfectly through eleven robberies, as most of the victims gladly surrendered their wallets and valuables, but when the Canadian man fought back, one of his attackers produced a gun and shot him execution style.

Now as Paul Harvey says, here's the rest of the story.

Fatima, the woman at the center of this story, was an acquaintance of yours truly. She was a troubled youth, and as we've already covered, I do like to keep my finger in the youth of America. The Prince and I had done a lot to support her, including

206

bailing her out of jail a handful of times, helping her through financial struggles, and getting her a good paying job at Steak and Shake.

Jim Cornette

I can assure you, Bolin has never given one dime to any man or woman in need. That's not to say he's lying when he claims to have lent a hand financially. He went out and found some sucker who had money and convinced them to lend the financial assistance.

Kenny

The Prince and I did everything we could for poor Fatima, but she was clearly running with a bad crowd and beyond our means to help. We lost track of her a while back when she moved to California, supposedly to do porn. I don't know if that's true, but when I saw her recently, she was in good spirits and seemed to be doing okay financially.

Fatima clearly didn't know what she was getting into with these two young men when they came up with their robbery scheme. They didn't set out to murder anyone, but a police detective friend of mine has told me that because of the role she played in the set up, she's just as guilty of murder as the trigger man.

Fatima and her partners were picked up after neighbors heard Fatima confessing the crime to anyone who would listen. She was clearly freaked out by the incident, as anyone would be. Someone called the police and less than 24 hours after the Canadian man died, Fatima and her co-conspirators were picked up by Louisville Metro police.

And here's the kicker: when the police searched their car, they found some Xanax pills, marijuana, a loaded Smith and Wesson, and two sets of Beets by Bolin headphones.

Yes, folks, a heinous murder was committed by a Beets customer, a known acquaintance of mine. A woman Jimmy Cornette once gave money too - at least I hope he tipped her, the cheap bastard!

Needless to say, demand for Beets has never been higher. Not to worry; I got into this business to provide a quality listening experience at a fraction of the cost, and while I have expanded to some higher end models, you will always be able to get my thug tested/ thug approved headphones at a fraction of what Apple charges for Beats.

Take that, Dr. Dre.

I'm sure many of you readers have had some fun at my expense. With each chapter, you've played a game, trying to guess when Kenny is telling the truth and when he is spinning a story. Contrary to popular belief, I do not make this shit up. Go back and listen to my podcasts They are for sale, if you would like a copy; just message me on Facebook. Listen to my stories. Listen to how consistent they are. What liar has ever ben able to keep a story straight every time they tell it??

No, sir, I am not lying to you when I tell you that I was friends with the King of Pop, Michael Jackson. Yes, THE Michael Jackson, native of Gary Indiana, brother of Tito and Jermaine and LaToya. Michael was a huge wrestling fan, as was his entire family, and during the days when OVW was the WWE developmental territory, I and several WWE and OVW stars were invited to the Neverland Ranch.

I didn't do a great deal of travel in my wrestling career by design, but the Neverland Ranch was by far the most amazing place I ever saw. It's truly a shame such a staggeringly beautiful and wondrous place is no longer open to anyone.

It was enjoyable getting to know Michael as well. Yes, I met Michael. I got to meet him at home, far from the spotlight of the paparazzi, where he was able to relax and be himself. I've met a great many celebrities in my time, and nothing compared to meeting Michael at the Neverland Ranch.

I've often said I'm the most famous person in wrestling never to be featured on national television. That maxim was proven true on June 25, 2009, the day my friend Michael Jackson passed away. Word of my travels to the Neverland Ranch and my friendship with Michael spread far and wide, and that evening, as the world struggled to come to grips with the news of Michael's death, I received a phone call from BBC News.

If you're not familiar with BBC News, it's the British equivalent of CNN, Fox, NBC, CBS, and ABC news all combined into one. It's that big and that powerful.

The BBC reached out to me to give the British people a sense of how we as Americans were dealing with the news of Michael's death. It was 5 AM when I went on the air to give the people of England the news from my point of view.

"How's America taking the news?" asked the BBC.

"Well, everyone's just been thrown for a loop," I said. "Everyone has their opinions about Michael Jackson. I heard the Reverend Al Sharpton remark how just a few weeks ago, no one even wanted to touch Michael Jackson because of past allegations. He's been in seclusion for so long, with no music and no concerts, it was like we were living without him already. Then he announced his concert dates at the O2 Arena. I was one of those who was excited to see him live again. Today feels a lot like the day Elvis died. You just feel like, 'No, no, this is Michael Jackson. He can't die.' That's how a lot of us feel right now."

"Tell me the mood in the states right now."

"Disbelief. I was at the Golden Corral just today, Golden Corral, and we were discussing Ed McMahon dying. We just lost Ed McMahon and Farrah Fawcett, and Shaquille O'Neal was just traded to Cleveland to play with Lebron James. We thought we had all the top news stories when someone walked over and told us that Michael Jackson was dead. We argued with him for twenty minutes until we went out to our cars and heard it for ourselves.

"It also reminds me of the day Andy Kaufman died. You think, 'Man, he'll do anything for publicity,' and you just wonder if he's really dead. People to this day still believe Elvis Presley is alive. They didn't want to believe it."

"What do you think the legacy of Michael Jackson will be, Kenny?" asked the reporter.

"I was just watching his CBS concert special from about 20 years ago. That was the one where he made that long entrance. He just stood there, no music, and put on the glove before me went into 'Billie Jean.' I remember thinking, 'Wow, what a performer. We're going to get to see this again.' And now, that's not going to happen."

"I suppose you have to pinch yourself to think that here you are, on BBC Radio, discussing the death of Michael Jackson."

"Well," I said, "It's not what I thought I'd be doing today, but I'm very pleased to be here on your show. Just like the rest of America, I can't believe it. I don't want to believe it. But it's obviously true."

John Cosper

I had just left dinner at a Golden Corral restaurant with Kenny Bolin and his mother when I heard this interview for the first time. Kenny played the interview in its entirety on Episode 26 of the Who's Slamming Who edition of the Bolin Alley. If I had not heard it with my own ears, I would not have believed it.

Kenny

It was a privilege and an honor, not only to know Michael, but to represent my country that evening speaking about his passing. It was a loss that truly hit home for me personally. We'd already lost the King of Rock and Roll Elvis, and shortly after we lost the King of Pop, we almost lost the King of Wrestling, Jerry Lawler, to an on-air heart attack.

Jerry's still with us, and the two of us are the only King's left. God save the Kings!

THE SAD SAGA OF LITTLE JIMMY LEBEAU

In late 2012 I had another very bad health scare. Over the previous twelve years I had gained thirty pounds a year, ballooning up to 569 pounds. That, coupled with my heart troubles, forced me to go to the hospital. It looked pretty serious, and doctors feared it might be the end of King B. My son called all of my friends and former clients, including Jim Cornette.

Four years earlier when I had a similar hospital scare, my son reached out to Jimmy, and the son of a bitch never came. I don't know what changed in the stretch between hospital stays, but this time, Jim actually showed his face in my room. It was truly nice to see there was still a heart beating inside his chest.

Jim Cornette

I showed up at the hospital, and Kenny tells me me has a duffel bag underneath him in the bed with five thousand dollars in cash! I said, "Kenny, what the hell are you doing with all that money?" He said, "Jim, do you think I'm just going to let it lie around my house where someone can steal it?"

Kenny was using the money to bribe the nurses to bring him sodas and candy bars. These doctors are trying to save his life, and he's undermining their work by eating junk food. I still don't know how he ever got out of that hospital.

Kenny

When a man has looked death in the face as I did, his thoughts turn from himself and back to those he stepped over on the way to the top. He thinks less about what he has left to conquer and more about how he might give back to those who weren't as fortunate as he. I'm not saying I'm done achieving in life; far from it. But you'd have to be a cold-hearted man not to stop and listen when someone comes to you with a story like the one I heard in the summer of 2014.

It was a lovely day at Bolin Manor when I got the phone call. I was reclining in my living room watching a University of Louisville football preview show with Ma Bolin beside me, feverishly applying decals to the latest shipment of Beets by Bolin headphones to work off her rent. The phone rang, and an unknown number with a Louisiana area code popped up.

"Hello," I said.

"Hello, is this Mr. Bolin?" It was a young man's voice with a thick Cajun accent.

"Yes, this is Kenny Bolin," I said. "How may I help you, son?"

The young man sighed. "You don't know how long I've waited for someone to call me that," he said.

"I beg your pardon?" I said.

"Oh, not you, sir," said the man. "I'm looking for my father, and my mother said you might be able to help me."

"Your mother told you to call me?" I said.

"Yes, sir. On her death bed."

Needless to say, I was intrigued. "Who is your mother?"

"Her name was Betty LeBeau," said the young man. "My name is James, but she always called me Little Jimmy."

"I'm very glad to know you, Little Jimmy," I said, "But I'm afraid the name Betty LeBeau doesn't ring a bell with me."

"No, sir," said Little Jimmy. "You don't know her, but she knows who you are. She says you and my Daddy were best friends at one time."

"Is that so?" I said.

"Yes, sir," said Little Jimmy. "She met my father at the Mid-South matches back in the 80s. She never told me who my Daddy was growing up, but on her death bed, she gave me his name and yours. She said you were a good man, and you would help me find my father."

As Little Jimmy told me his sad story, I thought back to the early 80s and who all was working for Mid-South Wrestling during that era. I had a good idea who this boy's father was, but I wanted to hear it for myself.

"Son," I said, "Who is your father?"

He swallowed hard, took a breath, and spoke the name. "Jim Cornette."

I nearly dropped the phone. Jim Cornette. My childhood best friend. My long-time nemesis. If I was driving down I-65 and saw a snake in one lane and Jim Cornette in the other, I'd plow over Jimmy, back up over him, and run him over again. I wanted to tell Little Jimmy what a lying, no good son of a bitch his old man was, but as I listened to Little Jimmy tell me how he grew up without a father, I started to think of my own son. I remember the good times we shared as he grew up before my eyes, all the memories I have that Jimmy never got to experience. I remembered, too, that Jim had come to see me this last time at the hospital. I thought about how much my son appreciates all the good memories we shared. I thought about the joyful times Jim and I had as young men, walking the rooftops with my television in hand, trying to pick up wrestling shows from far away.

Yes, Jim had done a lot to make me hate him in the ensuing years, but Jim was getting old. Real old. Hell, given his family history, he could be on his death bed any day now. Did I really want him to go and meet his Maker without at least attempting to patch up our differences?

I spoke to Little Jimmy a while longer, just to make sure this was no prank. He told me his birthday, and I looked it up online. Jim was out of the territory before Little Jimmy's birth, but he was still there nine months earlier when Little Jimmy was conceived. My heart went out to the young lad. I knew I had to help him connect with his father, but I knew Jim would never let it happen – not if it took place in private.

It's no secret that when I appear on Jim's podcast that his ratings go up dramatically. Jim knows this all too well, and even though he's loathe to bring me on, he'll do it to get those ratings. I contacted Jimmy and told him I would waive my usual fee for an appearance. I had something very important to get off my chest.

Jim Cornette

I got a call from Ma Bolin, begging me to let Kenny come on an upcoming show. Kenny had been in the hospital recently, and from what Ma Bolin told me, he had a pretty bad scare. She said Kenny had something important to say to me in front of all my listeners. Ma Bolin made it sound as if Kenny had a life-changing experience. I knew better than to believe that, having seen the bag of money he laid on the last time he was hospitalized, but because Ma Bolin begged me, I said yes.

As I expected, there was no change of heart in Kenny Starmaker Bolin. There wasn't even a real health scare. All he had was a bad case of indigestion! Kenny weaseled his way onto the program to ambush me with the biggest load of bullshit I have ever heard. He starts in with this story about Betty LeBeau, a woman I never met and never even heard of, and then he tells me that Betty's son Little Jimmy is my illegitimate child.

Next thing I know, my producer and I are on a four way call with Kenny and "Little Jimmy LeBeau." I have no idea who Little Jimmy is or what rock Kenny found him under, but he sounds like Adam Sandler in The Waterboy. Kenny keeps egging him on, trying to make me look like the jerk of the world in front of all my fans while Little Jimmy's telling me how much it hurts that I won't acknowledge him.

I've denied this story over and over at fan conventions and Q&A's ever since, but let me state it one more time for the record: I do not have a son. I do not know who Betty LeBeau is, and I do not know who Little Jimmy LeBeau is. Please stop asking, and please stop telling me I'm a bad father. Kenny Bolin brought that kid on my podcast for one reason only: somehow, some way, he is making a buck off Little Jimmy.

217

Kenny

It's sad, isn't it? You muster up the courage to do something good for someone who has done so much harm to you, and they throw it back in your face.

Little Jimmy's father continues to deny paternity, hiding behind the fortified walls of Castle Cornette while his son toils away at barely above minimum wage at the local Dairy Queen. One day the whole story will come out. I've already slipped Cosper a few Gattiland passes for his kids to start on a film adaptation of Little Jimmy's story. We've had talks with some big names out in LA, and if all goes well, Little Jimmy will make more money than his father ever did as the executive producer of Daddy Didn't Love Me: The Life Story of Little Jimmy LeBeau Cornette."

I know what Cornette is telling people about this project, but believe me, this is not for my own benefit. If Little Jimmy were my son, I couldn't sleep at night knowing that my son is working for peanuts while I live in the lap of luxury. Little Jimmy deserves his payday.

Now if Little Jimmy wants to cut his Uncle Kenny in for 40%, that's completely up to him.

Jerry Jarrett

I started hosting a podcast around the same time Kenny did for the same producer. I listened to Kenny's podcast, and I couldn't believe some of the things he would say about Jimmy. It finally got to the point that I called him up to discuss it.

"Listen," I said, "We all have our differences in this business, but I think you've been a bit hard on

Jimmy." I went on to try and tell him I thought he needed to let bygones be bygones, only to find out that it was all a work. Kenny and Jimmy have had endless fun reminding me how I bought into their heat.

I've been in the wrestling business my whole life. When I was five or six, I thought it was all real, but it hasn't been since I was fourteen that I believed what I saw. I had forgotten how it felt to be worked. Strange as it sounds, I really appreciated how Kenny was able to make me feel like that again.

A WORD FROM MY LOYAL SUBJECTS

It is an undisputed fact that there is only one king in Memphis, and his name is not Elvis.

Elvis may be the king of rock and roll, but in the city of Memphis, Jerry Lawler sits on the throne. It was his before Elvis left us, and he has never relinquished that crown. At one time, Memphis Wrestling had a higher rating within its viewing audience than any television show in America. Not even the fabled final episode of M*A*S*H could claim a higher share of viewers.

Jerry was beloved in Louisville, and he was a big reason why the Gardens was full all those Tuesday nights. But even Jerry Lawler would have to admit that in Louisville, I was the bigger man.

Jerry Lawler

Is Kenny still huge?

Kenny

While my time as King of OVW has past, there are parts of this town where I am still as beloved and treasured as ever. And while I may no longer be a television personality, don't you dare tell my loyal subjects that my reign has ended.

This chapter is dedicated to those people, specifically the ones who paid me for the privilege - dare I saw, the honor - of being included in my autobiography. Their comments are presented in chronological order of who submitted payment and are presented without editing or embellishment.

That's right, folks. These people paid good money to say these kind words about me.

Wayne Lauton of Milwaukee, formally from New Jersey. Always a Bolin Guy

Kenny found me in the Milwaukee, Wisconsin area and I became his #1 Bolin Guy in the mid-west, perhaps the nation, outside of his family.... Well, maybe even within. Who knows. He would have managed me if that was in the stars. In the meantime, he became a friend. Yep. Kenny Bolin. Maker of Stars. The Starmaker. Oh what could have been with him managing me. I would have named my finishing move "Now You See Stars By Bolin" and you would submit.

Jason Marshall, Stand Up Comic

I was doing a bit of self reflection on my journey into stand up comedy and I believe I owe you a big THANK YOU. In May of 2014 I sent you a message on Facebook and you forwarded it to Jim Cornette who read it on his show. I was thrilled! The very next Bolin Alley I called in for the first time. I was nervous to say the least. I called in every show until the show time changed. After that I wasn't able to call. But since then I was an in studio guest at a college radio station, the DJ liked me so much he kept me on for a full hour without going to break. After that he brought me back multiple times and I was asked to write for a local TV show. THANK YOU for having me on your show as a caller and preparing me for live radio.

Scott Cannon, Bolin fan

Although Kenny has had a successful career with the mega amount of stars he pushed up the ladder, it's still a shame to me the career he could have had if McMahon hadn't broken up the territories. He would have been one of the most known managerial talents in the business and Chris (the Prince) would have been known throughout the territories making a name of his own. Thanks again, McMahon, for ruining what once was a fun and enjoyable form of entertainment.

Cameron Forsythe, OVW fan

I grew up watching Ohio Valley Wrestling nearly every week as a kid with dreams of becoming a professional wrestler, even attended Christmas Chaos in 2001. Although I've only known Kenny Bolin personally for about 2 years, I've met his son Chris, even met the now elusive Ma Bolin. Throughout the numerous headphone sales and marketing ploys I still find myself saying, "I paid 79.95 for this?!" Yep, Starmaker got me again...he might've just screwed you too.

Andy Griffith, not from Mayberry

I am honored to be friends with Kenny Bolin. The Starmaker. Kenny is loyal to his friends and family even though he gives them hell at times but who doesn't? That's the way friends do one another. Kenny is the creator of Bolin Services and the longest reigning podcast, "The Bolin Alley" which I have been on and mentioned several times. Also Beets by Bolin which I have a few sets. I consider Kenny a good friend. GIVE EM HELL KING B!!!!!

Kyle Rieber, former OVW student and Bolin client

One of the best times we had with Kenny was at an OVW event at the Louisville Gardens. I can remember him wearing this purple suit with a yellow shirt. He look just like Barney the Dinosaur. A bunch of the guys from the firehouse and I were at the show that night so we decided to start singing the "I Love You, You Love Me" song to Kenny. That was one of the only times I can ever remember Kenny coming out of character as you couldn't help but laugh.

A few years later, I decided to wrestle in my first match. I was actually part of Bolin Services. That itself is pretty cool, but what was even cooler was that night, there was a newcomer to wrestling that was working his first night setting the ring up for my match. It was none other than the beast incarnate Brock Lesnar, who became a UFC champion and WWE Champion. I'm probably the only one that can claim that. Pretty cool.

Kenny, being true to form, found a way to get back at me for the Barney the Dinosaur song. If you want to find out what he did, I would suggest buying the Decade of Bolin DVD and checking it out. It's pure Kenny.

Paul RJ, Bolin fan from Down Under

How the hell did the WWE miss out on using this guy? Kenny has everything Pro Wrestling needs: talent, charisma, comic timing and the art of putting

Jim Cornette in his place. The only person who can turn Cornette into a blithering mess.

Cena and a lot of others owe 'Starmaker' Bolin a great debt of gratitude.

Tojo Yokohama, Number One Fan from Japan

Kenny Bolin is number one manager. I learn of Kenny from tapes I get from America. When I travel to Kentucky to see Kenny Bolin, he honor me by hitting me in head with briefcase. For me, to suffer concussion and compressed spine is number one. He further honor me by allowing me to buy dinner at Red Lobster for him, Prince, Mr. Black, and Rico-san. He thank me and honor me once more by clipping me with Cadillac as he drove off. Kenny Bolin number one manager. I am number one special fan.

Robert B.J. Puckett

Being a wresting fan, I met Kenny Bolin in 2013 after having a double hernia surgery and a rare Sarcoma surgery. When I rehabbed and was able to get back to work from this, I looked at a house he wanted to move into in Southern Indiana. The renovations would have been more than the house was worth, so we looked elsewhere and had a fish lunch in New Albany, Indiana. We went to lunch and talked, Kenny, the Prince, and me. I was sitting with celebrities and had the fortune to hear some road stories I always wanted to hear as a fan growing up.

We met a few more times after that, becoming friends and had a couple meals after that. I helped King B with a few odd jobs around his place fixing things, making plumbing repairs here and there as time allowed with a busy schedule. I even helped him move to his new location in Louisville while still on light duty.

I haven't seen King B in awhile due to work and family, but I'll never forget being able to meet him and the Prince and the chance to hear some classic road stories from the legend, the one and only Starmaker Kenny Bolin.

Now folks, I know you have probably been shaking your head throughout this book. You've read about my childhood and the scams and schemes and thought to yourself, this couldn't possibly be true. There's no way this man is for real about any of this. I can tell you two things: you are absolutely wrong, but you are not alone in thinking this is all BS.

This story comes courtesy of my old roommate, one of only three men to have ever held the OVW Heavyweight Championship, the OVW Southern Tag Title, and the OVW Television Championship. No, it's not CM Punk or Jamin Olivencia, but my old buddy Aron "The Idol" Stevens. You probably know him as Damien Sandow, or Damien Mizdow, Macho Mizdow, or whatever gimmick he's selling the hell out of (and getting over with!) this week.

Aron Stevens

Wrestlemania 2015 was in Los Angeles. I was still working as the Miz's stunt double, and one night Miz and I were told we were going out to a big Hollywood party. The two of us and a couple of other WWE Superstars were taken out by limo to this mansion in the hills, a bigger place than any of us had ever seen. The only thing more amazing than the house were the faces we saw milling around inside. These were big name Hollywood stars. We had no idea why they wanted a couple of WWE wrestlers to walk among them, but we weren't going to argue.

Miz and I were approached by a couple of guys from the *Hot Tub Time Machine* movies. They were big fans of ours and were really excited to see us. We got to chatting about Wrestlemania for a bit, and then something happened I never in a million years saw coming.

"So we have a question for you," one of them asked. "Both of you guys worked with Kenny Bolin, right?"

Miz and I were both taken aback. "Yes," we said.

"He managed both of you?"

"Yes, he did," we said. "How do you guys know about Kenny?"

"We've heard him on the Bolin Alley and on The Jim Cornette Experience," they told us. "We're big fans. We love the show, but all that stuff he talks about... that's not for real is it? I mean, he couldn't really be the way he acts on the podcasts, right?"

I laughed and pointed at some nearby seats. "Sit down, all of you. This is going to take a while."

I started to tell them all about Kenny. I told them about the meat scam, the insurance scams. I told them about the time we ate for free for two solid weeks. I told them story after story. Things Kenny told me, things I saw with my own eyes. Miz got bored of it and wandered away. I think he was annoyed that everyone was more interested in hearing about Bolin than himself.

Finally I got to the story about Kenny's brother Biscuits and Gravy and how he lived with Colonel

Harland Sanders for a year. That was enough for them.

"This is all bullshit," they said. "You're working us, there's no way, no way any of this could be true!"

I swore to them it was the honest to goodness truth. "If you say it's true, we'll believe you," they said as we all shook hands. I don't think they believed me, but they still seemed to appreciate the story.

When I was at OVW, I never dreamed I'd end up at a big Hollywood party, and the last thing I expected to hear at that party was the name Kenny Bolin. But as Kenny would say, hand to God, I spent half an hour at a Hollywood party telling the cast of *Hot Tub Time Machine* the very strange but true story of Kenny Bolin's life.

Kenny

As we go to press, I don't have any news to share as a follow up to this story, but you may already be hearing rumblings about the Starmaker doing a cameo in an upcoming sequel. It will take an awfully big number, and an awfully big hot tub, but just like the wrestling business, you can never say never when it comes to Hollywood!

I've been out of the wrestling business for several years now, but you never truly get it out of your system. I still dream about it, and in dreaming, I still cut promos in my sleep. The odd thing is if I wake up in the middle of a promo, I finish it out loud. Or so I am told.

One night not too long ago, I had a dream I was cutting a promo about The Rock. The Rock had already come out to the ring and cut a promo about me. He told everyone all the things I had done for the wrestling business, all the lessons I had taught, all the careers I helped to launch. The Rock said I was a legend, and I deserved to be treated as such, so he had bought me a house – 117 West Main Street in LaGrange, Kentucky. For those of you who skipped my early life stories to get to the wrestling stuff, that's the shithouse apartment I grew up in.

The Rock said he was moving me and my mother back into 117 West Main. Not only that, The Rock said he would be living in the apartment himself whenever he was in town, as if The Rock would ever have reason to come to LaGrange, Kentucky.

After The Rock finished, I got in the ring and picked up the mic. "I can't believe this. I can't believe what I'm hearing. To hear, that you, The Rock would come out here and say all these nice things about me. It means a lot. I really does. But then, you go, and you buy me not just a house, but 117 West Main Street. You, The Rock, who made 42 million dollars last year.

You, The Rock, who has millionaire friends like Stone Cold Steve Austin and John Cena, who owes me far more than you do for the millions he's earned. You have all that money, and all those rich friends, and you buy me that house? That house only cost us $100 a month rent when we moved in. It cost barely more than that when we moved out. It couldn't possibly cost more than $300 a month now, if that! And you, The Rock, with all your money and rich friends want to stick me and Ma Bolin back in that apartment?"

The next morning, Ma Bolin asked me, "Kenny, were you mad at The Rock in your dream last night?"

I thought about it and I said, "Yes I was. Why?"

"Because you were saying some terrible things about him in your sleep last night."

I told her exactly why I had said all those awful things about The Rock. She understood completely. I wouldn't go back to 117 West Main Street in LaGrange for anything, and I would only wish such a fate on a select few of my worst enemies. You can probably guess who is at the top of that list.

Crybaby Chris Alexander, former OVW wrestler

I used to play a lot of acoustic gigs with a friend of mine, just two guys and our guitars. We did a lot of late nights at restaurants around Louisville and Southern Indiana. One night we were playing in an Applebees on the south side of Louisville. They had us set up on a nice little stage in the restaurant. Just as we were about to start playing, I looked up and started laughing. Over the stage, on the wall amid all the other random pieces of nostalgia, was a signed photo of Kenny Bolin looking down on us.

Kenny

There are some who say I cast a large shadow, and not just the ones who call me obese. I may be out of the wrestling business, but Kenny Bolin is still alive and well, enjoying the support of my fans and the success of my current business endeavors.

Jim Cornette

Back in early 2009 we had a terrible ice storm in the Louisville area. The ice caused all sorts of damage, and about half the city lost power. Many people went up to two weeks before they could get power restored to their homes!

Like most Louisville natives, I had to sit in the dark for a few days. But not Kenny! I found out after the fact that he had weaseled his way into a room at the five star Galt House Hotel downtown with his two dogs!

Not only that, but Kenny got his power switched on early by bribing some of the fine men who work for Louisville Gas and Electric. He went out for a drive and spotted a bunch of LG&E trucks in the parking lot at Golden Corral. He parked his car, opened the trunk, and pulled out a bunch of his 8 x 10 photos and bootleg John Cena DVDs. A few autographed photos and DVDs later, Bolin's got a truck headed to his house, jumping him in front of thousands patiently waiting to get power.

What's worse, Kenny is right up the street from the Home of the Innocents, a local shelter house for kids in crisis. These troubled kids are sitting in the dark freezing while Kenny and his damn dogs sit and enjoy the heat, just a few blocks away.

Kenny

Jimmy loves to try and make me look bad. He always has. But let's get something straight. I've done more than my share for the youth of America. For years, I raised money through my own charitable trust, the Bolin fund, to give assistance to teenage girls, ages 14-16, in need of a little fatherly guidance. Just like our motto says, I have my finger in the youth of America.

And as for Home of the Innocents, hell, I've supported those kids many times. Over the years I must have given thousands of dollars in free autographed photos to those kids, just to brighten their day.

So how am I a bad person for looking out for me and my two dogs? There were about 137 kids at that home in the winter of 2009, plus another dozen or so adults working as staff. Do you know what kind of body heat 137 people can create, huddled together? There's 137 of them. There's only one of me. Think what a tragic loss that would have been for Louisville if I had not survived that storm.

Sometimes the needs of the few, or the one, do outweigh the needs of the many.

Sylvester Terkay

Kenny's always had a soft spot for animals, and he always had a few pets. He had a cat that he named after me, Sylvester, meanest old alley cat you ever saw. This cat was so mean, it literally chased off every other cat in the apartment complex where Kenny lived.

One of the other tenants in the apartment complex let his two pit bulls get loose one day. The dogs came after Sylvester. The cat beat up on the dogs, and they never messed with him again.

Of course it was against the rules for anyone in the apartment complex to have pets, but when the cat's reputation became known, the apartment manager decided Sylvester was an asset to the community and let him stay.

Nova

I was there the night Kenny met his now daughter-in-law Mayara. She had just arrived in America, and Chris had taken her around town to introduce her to family. Kenny was last, and he insisted Chris bring her out to dinner - at the Golden Corral, where he was selling his T-shirts, DVDs, and headphones.

Chris walks in with this lovely young lady and introduces her to his father. Kenny, ever the showman, stands up and introduces her to me, his mother, John Cosper, and Big Frank, one of Kenny's long time friends and fans. Before she can even sit down, he's got a pair of Beets by Bolin headphones on her head, and he's trying to pull thirty bucks out of her. The man is a living gimmick.

Kenny

Christopher and his new bride Mayara are both in college. They're here in Louisville for now, but they have hopes of moving back to Mayara's home country of Germany. Chris is now, by marriage, a citizen of both the United States and Germany.

Chris continues to do well in his career. He took on a number of challenges after leaving Central States, and he currently works for one of Louisville's largest and most prestigious companies as a food distribution coordinator.

Jim Cornette

Catbox isn't an executive. He's a delivery boy for Pizza Hut, a brand owned by Louisville-based Yum! Corporation. His "take home" may be better than most, but I can assure you the apple did not fall far from the tree with this boy. One afternoon I was eating with Kenny, John, and Dean Hill at a Chili's located right next to Catbox's Pizza hut store. When Catbox found out we were there, he began dropping in on us in between deliveries, mooching wings and fries while finagling a Diet Pepsi and several refills out of our hard-working waiter.

Kenny

As much as I've enjoyed watching my son and his wife start their new life together, they've brought me a few headaches, specifically in the form of small animals. We are all lovers of animals in the Bolin household (my brother's past history with fighting cocks notwithstanding), so when Mayara brought home an adorable puppy, I of course opened my home to the beast. And no, contrary to what come would claim, I did not charge him rent.

I should have charged him something, because as I soon found out, this dog has a nose for money. One day I left my bag of movies and Beets by Bolin headphones in the middle of the living room. I also left my wallet, filled with credit cards, cash, Gattiland coupons, and Golden Corral coupons which, let's face it, are just as good as currency.

Now this dog Mayara brought home had already proven to be a bit of a pain, sticking his nose places it did not belong, but this particular day, he really crossed the line. I came into the living room and discovered a complete mess. All of my movies were out of the bag, scattered to the four corners. It looked like he had chewed up at least half my inventory. What's worse, the little bastard also got into my wallet. Hand to God, all the Gattiland coupons, Golden Corral coupons, and credit cards were gone, along with all of the big bills. All that was left inside the were a few ones and fives!

I called Mayara and let her know that the dog she and Chris had brought into my home, the dog I had welcomed out of the kindness of my heart, was about to go to the shelter. It wasn't just that the dog got into the bag. It wasn't just that it chewed up a few things. It selectively managed to devour the most valuable items inside my wallet. If I didn't know any better, I'd have sworn that Jim Cornette had something to do with that dog manipulating its way into my home.

Well, now we come to the most astonishing part of the saga. It seems the dog heard me planning to take it to a shelter, where goodness knows when or whether it would ever find another home, much less a home as nice as mine. The next day, out of nowhere, the coupons, the credit cards, and the big bills appeared in the dog's bed, all intact, unchewed, undamaged. Matter of fat, the big bills all appear to have been sorted. I can't prove anything because I didn't actually see the dog with the money, but my suspicion is the dog had plans to make off with the money and start a new life on the nest egg he nearly embezzled from me.

Hand to God, it's the truth.

Dean Hill

I used to get real worried when Kenny said, "Hand to God." He says it a lot, and whenever he said it at OVW, I'd take a step away, afraid that God might actually strike him down with lightning. Now I don't worry so much. I figure as large as Kenny is, God shouldn't have any trouble hitting his target.

John Bradshaw Layfield

Kenny has an incredible gift of gab and is very talented. I have had some great times with Kenny. He's very self deprecating in person which most intelligent people have that gift to make everyone comfortable just like Kenny does. I enjoyed being around Kenny because he understands sports entertainment on a ground level, the basic level of entertainment - good versus evil and who wants to be the good guy, because us bad guys have all the fun. On this we both agreed and had a shared love of our business. He managed a bunch of the greats before they became great. I was just glad he didn't eat them.

Sylvester Terkay

I became friends with some of the other guys at OVW, but it was complicated. We were friendly, but we were also each other's competition. We were all fighting to get a WWE roster spot. Kenny was a real friend to me while I was there. He was always good with advice, and he had an ear to the ground to let me know what was going on. He took good care of me.

Mark Henry

Kenny Bolin is like many people in pro wrestling or sports entertainment. They believe in what they do, it's the only way to make it. Suspend disbelief! The reason King Bolin worked for so long is that he really is Kenny Bolin! Every now and then Kenny would rub me the wrong way. I had to regroup and say that's him being him! He played his role then and plays it now. Just go out with him and you will see!

Terry Garvin Simms

Kenny Bolin doesn't put up with B.S. Kenny Bolin is B.S., and that stands for Bolin Services.

Kenny

If you go to OVW on a Wednesday night for their weekly TV taping, you won't see me at the announcer's desk. You won't see my son Chris walking out of the locker rooms with any clients either. Both of us are now retired, and the way we left things, doubt if either of us ever return to OVW.

That said, if you go to the Golden Corral on a Taylorsville Road in Louisville on a Thursday evening, you'll find me and an assortment of friends and fans just about every week. I have a tradition now known as "Beets and Eats by Bolin" where I treat a few fans to dinner in exchange for the purchase of a few T-shirts and headphones.

John Cosper

One evening, while I was going through the arduous task of proofing this book, I received a voice mail from Kenny. He had dialed my number by mistake, and he thought he was leaving a message for one of his many Beets by Bolin customers about an upcoming visit to Golden Corral. The voice mail gave me a rare insight into the real Kenny Bolin as he spoke about a young fan, a girl with autism, who would be his dinner guest along with his family. He was treating all four of them to dinner and hooking the young lady up with a pair of Beets, and autographed photo, and a copy of a John Cena video.

It's entirely possible that once this young girl got to the restaurant, Kenny charged her for her stuff just the same as he did his own daughter-in-law the night he met her, but I prefer to think that there actually is a heart underneath all that bravado. As Jim Cornette likes to say, you just have to dig through too many layers to get to it.

Kenny

Regardless of what my haters say, the King still reigns in Louisville. I'm well known about town, and I've become a much sought after guest in the realm of wrestling podcasts. Sure, I might have cut a few corners in my day, on my behalf and on behalf of my clients. And yes, I probably screwed a few people over, including those same clients. I probably screwed you too at some point. But when you've been screwed by Kenny Bolin, you've been screwed by the very best. Consider it an honor - nay, a privilege that it happened. Now you too can tell your friends, your children, and your grandchildren that you have a story to tell about the legendary Starmaker, Kenny "The King" Bolin.

Good day. I SAID, good day!!

AFTERWORD BY RICO COSTANTINO

I got an email inviting me to call in and participate in a Roast of Kenny Bolin on Blogtalkradio. I was a little late calling in, thanks to some perps who have no respect for my time as a member of Las Vegas law enforcement, and I was afraid I would miss my chance to participate. Luckily, the broadcast went beyond its 90 minute scheduled run, and I was able to get on at about the two hour point. I know people wanted to hear me roast Kenny for all the things he did to me back in OVW, but I couldn't do it. My years at OVW were golden, and King B, the Round Mound of Sound, my Big Blue M&M, was the biggest part of that, figuratively and literally.

I was the first WWE talent assigned to OVW. When I arrived, they were surprised to learn I was already 38 years old. They really did think I was 25. Still, my resume as an American Gladiators made me star material, and Cornette pushed me as the top babyface right away.

Then at a Louisville Gardens show, I tore my quad in a match against the Andretti boys. OVW and the WWE were supportive of me during my recovery, but I really didn't know what was going to happen.

That's when King B came into my life in a big way. He went to Cornette and asked what the plans were when I returned. Jim wanted to push me as a babyface, a good guy, when I came back. But Kenny had different ideas.

"Make him a heel," he said.

"No!" said Cornette.

"Give me six weeks," said Kenny. "I'll make him bigger as a heel than he ever was as a face."

Kenny did exactly what he said he would. In a triple threat match for the OVW title, I smashed fan favorite Flash Flanigan in the back with a steel chair and aligned myself with Bolin Services. I went from being the top babyface to the top heel in one night. Then Kenny and I brought in John Cena as my tag team partner, the Prototype. We were huge, and Kenny was the man who made it happen.

Life with Kenny Bolin was pretty much what you've read in these pages. We ate all over Louisville: Steak and Shake, Kingfish, Applebees, Hooters, you name it. We never paid for a meal. Kenny knew how to barter, and he really took care of me and the boys.

I got a little upset with Kenny one time. When I became part of Bolin Services, Kenny asked me to sign a bunch of 8x10 photos for him. We were out at a restaurant one night, and when Kenny opened his trunk, there were my photos tossed all over the place.

"What the hell is this?" I yelled. I had trusted him to help push and promote me all over town. Kenny explained that this was how he worked, out of the back of his car. I didn't believe him. I really wondered if he was selling drugs or something!

But over time I began to understand Kenny. Kenny used our photos to put us over everywhere he went. Yes, he used them as currency to buy meals, but he was also spreading the word about John Cena, Rico Constantino, and the rest of Bolin Services.

Kenny did more than put us over. He took care of us. He wasn't just feeding himself; he was buying our meals, too, like the night I paid that $100 tab with a kiss at Kingfish. He invited us into his home, and we all became like family.

There's no doubt in my mind King B could have been a huge star. He had the talent on the mic, and he had a great mind for the business. But Kenny never, ever put himself ahead of us. Everything he did was for his boys. He's one of the most unselfish people I know. That may surprise people to hear, but he really does put other people first.

Before I was with Bolin, I met a boy who became a big fan of mine. He had cerebral palsy, and every week, he had to go to physical therapy. It was a very hard, very painful thing for him to endure, but after I got to know him, I started spending an hour a week with him at therapy. It meant a lot to me and to him.

As a babyface, I always played to my young friend. I nodded to him and acknowledged him in the ring, and after every match, I took off my wristband and gave it to him. When I became a part of Bolin Services, I couldn't do all of that. I had to be a heel, and I had to ignore him. But Kenny knew what that child meant to me, and what I meant to him, and he allowed me to continue handing off my wristband after every match. I never forgot that.

Kenny Bolin could have been selfish. He could have put himself over us, and he could have made himself the star. Instead, Kenny Bolin turned us into stars. Everything I achieved at OVW and the WWE, I owe to Kenny Bolin. He made me the biggest heel at OVW, and he made me someone the WWE wanted to put on Raw and Smackdown.

I was very blessed to do the things I did, and I am thankful to say that Kenny Bolin is still my friend.

He's the most generous, unselfish man I have every known, and I thank him for my career.

I love you, King B.

Rico Costantino
June 7, 2015

APPENDIX A: BOLIN SUCCESS STORIES

In the fourteen years I worked at OVW, I helped to groom and prepare dozens of men and women for the bright lights of the WWE. The following is as complete a list as my memory could compile of the folks I personally helped along the way.

Some became stars. Others, for various reasons, didn't last. One became arguably the biggest star of all time. All of them have me to thank for the success they had, however meager.

John Cena
Rico Costantino
Bull Buchanan
Mark Henry
Sean O'Haire
Nova
The Big Show
Damien Sandow
Lance Cade
Mark Jindrak
Gene Snitsky
Bobby Lashley
Sylverter Terkay
Nick Dinsmore
Rob Conway
Rene Dupree

Ken Doane
The Miz
Mike Mondo
Bam Neely
Cassidy Riley
JTG
Carlito

Bolin Services clients also won a combined total of 37 championships. Those champions include:

OVW Champions:
John Cena
Rico Constantino (3 times)
Rob Conway (3 times)
Nick Dinsmore (8 times)

OVW Television Champions:
Ken Doane
Rocco Bellagio

OVW Southern Tag Team Champions
Mr. Black & Bull Buchanan
Rico Constantino & The Prototype
Nick Dinsmore & Rob Conway (10 times)
Mike Mizanin & Chris Cage
K.C. & Kassidy James (4 times)
Charles Evans & Justin LaRouche
James Thomas & Rocco Bellagio

OVW Hardcore Champion:
Mr. Black

APPENDIX B: BOLIN'S WOMEN

A gentleman does not brag about his conquests. I am no gentleman, but then again, I'm not one to share everything about my damn personal life.

Many people have asked just how many wrestling divas have graced my bed. I won't name names, but in the interest of giving the fans a piece of what they want, here are the names of a few that I did NOT sleep with. The rest I leave to your lurid imaginations to figure out.

Mae Young
Linda McMahon
Vickie Guerrero
Synn
Jackie Gayda

APPENDIX C: EAT LIKE A KING

I'm a well known figure around Louisville, and yes, I have certain establishments that I prefer to frequent due to long standing relationships with management, ownership, and such. If you want to eat like a King, then here are the places you can sample my favorite meals and - if you're lucky - stumble into a chance meeting with myself and some of my known associates.

Clarksville Seafood,

Eastern Boulevard in Clarksville, IN

It's true, I don't care much for Indiana, but I will cross the bridge for this legendary establishment featuring the best seafood in the area. I usually get two fish dinners with fries when I am there. The homemade tartar sauce is excellent.

Golden Corral

Taylorsville Road

Like all Golden Corral restaurants, this one is now a buffet, but the king prefers the fried fish over the steak most nights.

Applebees

Bardstown Road

Dinner of choice: the pineapple burger.

Steak N Shake

Bardstown Rd and Hurstbourne Lane

Try the triple cheese burger with a peanut butter shake.

Hooters

Preston Hwy and Dupont Circle

All-u-can-eat boneless chicken with honey mustard.

Gattiland

Outer Loop

This one used to have two locations. Sadly, the LaGrange Road store is now closed. When you go, ask for the Kenny Bolin special: all the meats except ham with extra cheese, mushrooms, tomatoes, peppers, and onions.

Raising Canes

Bardstown Road

This place has only been open a short while, but the King is already in with the owners. I order the Caniac with two extra chicken fingers and two kaiser rolls with lettuce along with extra fries, slaw, honey mustard, and Texas toast.

Mark's Feed Store

Shelbyville Road

This isn't one of my places, but it's Cornette's favorite place in town. I'm always happy to go of course - so long as someone else is buying. The original store on Shelbyville Road used to be an actual feed store. If you want to eat like Cornette, try the burgoo, but if you want a feast for a King, get the catfish.

Qdoba

1500 Bardstown Rd

The King's feast usually orders the naked burrito loaded with ground beef, pico de gallo, rice, cheese, beans and guacamole. I'll follow that up with a loaded chicken quesadilla.

Mc Donalds

Fegenbush Lane off of Bardstown Road

The Double Quarter Pounder with Cheese with extra pickles and onions.

APPENDIX D: THANK YOUS

My friend John Cosper advised me I should give thanks to the people who legitimately contributed to this book. For those who are curious, here's a list of those who gave quotes for this book (or were quoted from other sources).

"The Prince" Christopher Bolin
"Crybaby" Chris Alexander
Bill Apter
Rick Brady
Mike "Nova" Bucci
Jim Cornette
Rico Costantino
Mark Cuban
Tim Denison
Mark Henry
Dean Hill
Jerry Jarrett
Jim Kurnau
Jerry "The King" Lawler
John Bradshaw Layfield
"Dirty" Dutch Mantell
"The Sinister Minister" James Mitchell
Mad Man Pondo
Bishop Jason Sanderson

Terry Garvin Simms
Christian Skyfire
Al Snow
Aron "The Idol" Stevens (aka Damien Sandow)
Sylvester Terkay

And here, once again, are my fans/benefactors who were honored enough to pay for the privilege of seeing their words about me in print:

Wayne Lauton
James Marshall
Scott Cannon
Cameron Forsythe
Andy Griffith
Kyle Rieber
Paul RJ
Robert B.J. Puckett

Special thanks to Christopher J. Longenecker for designing one incredible book cover after another.

Special thanks as well to my son Christopher, my daughter-in-law Mayara, my attorney Tim Denison, and frenemy for life, Jim Cornette.

ABOUT JOHN COSPER

John Cosper is a good friend of mine and the author of *Bluegrass Brawlers: The Story of Professional Wrestling in Louisville*. It's an okay book, but he spends too little time on me and too much time talking about men who didn't do as much for this business as I did like Jerry Lawler, Jerry Jarrett, John Cena, CM Punk, Lou Thesz, Ed "Strangler" Lewis, and Jimmy Cornette. When John isn't stuffing his face on fish at Clarksville Seafood thanks to my generosity, he's probably writing something else about wrestling or spending time with his family. His website is www.eatsleepwrestle.com if you give a crap.

ABOUT KENNY BOLIN

If you want to know about the author of this book, buy the damn book and read it. It's called an autobiography. The entire book is about the author. So if you think I'm gonna give even one thing away for free on the back page of this book, you're even more ignorant than Danny Inferno.

Want to know more about wrestling in Louisville? Read my friend's book!

Yes, sir, 130 and some odd years worth of wrestling stories from the River City. You'll read out "Strangler" Lewis became the Strangler, and learn what other future world champions cut their teeth in my town before my boy John Cena. And of course, you get to read about me. Featuring a foreword by Jim Cornette and an Afterword by yours truly, Bluegrass Brawlers is a must read for Louisville wrestling fans. Available on Amazon.com.

Want to be my friend? Want to get a pair of Beets?
Answer the second question first, then find me on the
web at:

http://www.facebook.com/starmakerbolin